Pitfalls of Christian Liberty

Pitfalls of Christian Liberty

by
John MacArthur, Jr.

WORD OF GRACE COMMUNICATIONS
P.O. Box 4000
Panorama City, CA 91412

Library of Congress Cataloging in Publication Data

MacArthur, John, 1939-
Pitfalls of Christian liberty.

(John MacArthur's Bible series)
Includes indexes.
1. Bible. N.T. Corinthians, 1st X, 1-22
—Criticism, interpretation, etc. I. Title.
II. Series: MacArthur, John, 1939-
Bible studies.
BS2675.2.M285 1988 227'.207 88-1532
ISBN 0-8024-5360-0

1 2 3 4 5 6 7 Printing/LC/Year 93 92 91 90 89 88

Printed in the United States of America

Contents

These Bible studies are taken from messages delivered by Pastor-Teacher John MacArthur, Jr., at Grace Community Church in Panorama City, California. These messages have been combined into a 5-tape album entitled *Pitfalls of Christian Liberty.* You may purchase this series either in an attractive vinyl cassette album or as individual cassettes. To purchase these tapes, request the album *Pitfalls of Christian Liberty,* or ask for the tapes by their individual GC numbers. Please consult the current price list; then, send your order, making your check payable to:

WORD OF GRACE COMMUNICATIONS
P.O. Box 4000
Panorama City, CA 91412

Or call the following toll-free number:
1-800-55-GRACE

1
The Danger of Overconfidence—Part 1

Outline

Introduction
- A. The Limitations of Liberty
  - 1. The evidence of the problem
    - *a*) Conflict
    - *b*) Compromise
  - 2. The essence of the problem
- B. The Danger of Overconfidence
  - 1. Illustrated in the Old Testament
    - *a*) Haman
    - *b*) Nebuchadnezzar
    - *c*) The Edomites
  - 2. Illustrated in the New Testament
    - *a*) Peter
    - *b*) The Corinthians

Lesson
- I. The Assets of Liberty (vv. 1-4)
  - A. Being Liberated by God's Power (v. 1)
    - 1. Domination
    - 2. Deliverance
    - 3. Designation
    - 4. Disqualification
  - B. Being Labeled as God's People (v. 2)
    - 1. The rite
      - *a*) Confusion
      - *b*) Clarification
    - 2. The reality
      - *a*) The symbolism examined
      - *b*) The significance explained

C. Being Showered with God's Provision (vv. 3-4)
   1. The source (v. 3)
   2. The sustenance (vv.3-4*a*)
   3. The Sustainer (v. 4*b*-*c*)

II. The Abuses of Liberty (vv. 5-10)
   A. Stated (v. 5)
      1. The extent
      2. The explanation
      3. The examination
   B. Summarized (v. 6)
      1. Loathing God's provision
      2. Lusting for the past
      3. Learning from God's purification

Introduction

First Corinthians deals with practical problems in the church, one of which was determining what to do in areas the Bible doesn't address. The Bible says that certain things are right and certain things are wrong, but it doesn't say anything about many other areas. How can a Christian know what to do in situations not mentioned in the Bible? We often call those matters "gray areas." From chapter 8 through the first verse of chapter 11 Paul discusses the answer to that question.

In chapter 8 Paul emphasizes that a Christian has liberty in gray areas. If an action isn't wrong, he has the moral right to do it. Two things should determine whether he does it: how it affects others and how it affects himself. In chapter 9 Paul describes how our liberty can affect others by using an illustration from his life. In chapter 10 he uses Israel to illustrate how abusing liberty can bring you into temptation and sin, ultimately disqualifying you from service for Christ.

A. The Limitations of Liberty

1. The evidence of the problem

a) Conflict

The Corinthian Christians believed they were free to do whatever they wanted because they had been saved, instructed in the Word of God, and granted spiritual gifts. They believed that their maturity permitted them to participate in questionable activities without being affected.

But weaker Christians in the Corinthian church recognized that some of the things other believers felt free to do, they could not do. For example, a man recently saved out of idolatry watches a mature Corinthian go to the temple of an idol and eat a meal with his friends. The recent convert knows that if he were to go, he would become too attached to his former life-style. Therefore he confronts the mature Christian about his participation in idolatry. The mature Christian responds, "I ignore the idolatry; I just eat the food." But the weaker Christian can't separate the two. Paul said to consider that your actions can affect others—that someone could be caused to sin by following your example.

In our society you may find a gray area that you can handle. But a weaker Christian, trusting your discernment, might follow your example and end up returning to the sin he was saved from. Finding himself compromised, he would think less of you as a Christian and never understand how you could participate freely.

b) Compromise

In 1 Corinthians 9:27 Paul says, "I keep under my body, and bring it into subjection, lest that by any means, when I have preached to others, I myself should be a castaway [disqualified]." Paul recognized that although he was actively serving God, if he didn't discipline himself, he could overstep his liberty, fall into temptation and sin, and be disqualified from serving Christ. You can't stretch your liberty to its limit without the danger of falling into sin. The smug Corinthian who went to the festival claimed that his only interests were the food and the social contact. He said he ignored the idolatry and the orgies. Doubting that claim, Paul said it would be better to avoid all appearance of evil and not to have to face the resulting temptation (v. 27).

2. The essence of the problem

The basic problem is overconfidence. When a Christian becomes so confident of his maturity that he believes he can't fall, he is in a precarious position. Verse 12, the crux of verses 1-11, says, "Let him that thinketh he standeth take heed lest he fall."

B. The Danger of Overconfidence

The Bible warns about overconfidence. Proverbs 16:18 says, "Pride goeth before destruction, and an haughty [proud] spirit before a fall." Proverbs 29:23 says, "A man's pride shall bring him low." Repeatedly in the Bible God humbles the proud. Let's look at some illustrations of overconfidence and see how God dealt with it.

1. Illustrated in the Old Testament

a) Haman

Esther was a beautiful Jewish woman living in the Persian kingdom. The Persian king Ahasuerus (also called Xerxes) became angry at his wife Vashti because during a festival he commanded her to come so that he might display her beauty. But she refused, knowing he was drunk and that he probably wanted to disrobe her before everyone (Esther 1:10-12). The wise men, recognizing that the example of the queen might lead other women in the kingdom to disobey their husbands, recommended that Vashti be deposed (vv. 15-19). The king accepted their advice (v. 21). Then he demanded that a search begin for a new queen (2:2-4), and eventually he selected Esther (v. 17). But he had some anti-Semitic subjects, particularly one man named Haman, who plotted to kill all the Jews (3:6). Haman even built a gallows at his house to hang Esther's adoptive father, Mordecai (5:14).

When the king discovered, however, that Mordecai had thwarted a plot to assassinate him, he decided to honor him (6:1-3). As the king was considering how to honor Mordecai, Haman came to request his death. Before he could make his request, the king asked Haman, "What shall be done for the man whom the king delighteth to honor? Now Haman thought in his heart, To whom would the king delight to do honor more than to myself? And Haman answered the king . . . Let the royal apparel be brought which the king is accustomed to wear, and the horse that the king rideth upon, and the crown royal which is set upon his head; and let this apparel and horse be delivered to the hand of one of the king's most noble princes, that they may array the man whom the king delighteth to honor, and bring him on horseback through the street of the city" (6:6-9). When Haman finished, the king basically said, "Go do that for Mordecai" (v. 10). Later, when the king heard about Haman's plot, he had Haman hanged on his own gallows (7:10). That's the danger of overconfidence.

b) Nebuchadnezzar

Nebuchadnezzar, king of Babylon, believed he was invincible. Daniel 4:30-33 says that "the king spoke, and said, Is not this great Babylon, that I have built for the house of the kingdom by the might of my power, and for the honor of my majesty? While the word was in the king's mouth, there fell a voice from heaven, saying, O King Nebuchadnezzar, to thee it is spoken, The kingdom is departed from thee. And they shall drive thee from men, and thy dwelling shall be with the beasts of the field; they shall make thee to eat grass like oxen, and seven times shall pass over thee, until thou know that the Most High ruleth in the kingdom of men, and giveth it to whomsoever he will. The same hour was the thing fulfilled upon Nebuchadnezzar, and he was driven from men, and did eat grass like oxen, and his body was wet with the dew of heaven, till his hairs were grown like eagles' feathers, and his nails like birds' claws."

c) The Edomites

The book of Obadiah is a prophecy against Edom, an area southeast of Israel. Petra, the greatest city in Edom, was carved out of cliffs in a canyon. There was only one entrance to Petra, and it was so well designed that one man could defend it.

So the Edomites were confident that they were invincible. God replied, "The pride of thine heart hath deceived thee, thou who dwellest in the clefts of the rock . . . who saith in his heart, Who shall bring me down to the ground? Though thou exalt thyself like the eagle, and though thou set thy nest among the stars, from there will I bring thee down" (Obad. 3-4). God did destroy the city, and today only animals and birds occupy it.

2. Illustrated in the New Testament

a) Peter

Jesus, shortly before He was betrayed, told His disciples, "All ye shall be offended because of me this night; for it is written, I will smite the shepherd, and the sheep of the flock shall be scattered abroad. But after I am raised up again, I will go before you into Galilee. Peter answered and said unto him, Though all men shall be offended because of thee, yet will I never be offended. Jesus said unto him, Verily I say unto thee that this night, before the cock crows, thou shalt deny me thrice" (Matt. 26:31-34; cf. Zech. 13:7).

b) The Corinthians

First Corinthians 10:1-13 tells us the Corinthians were smug. They were confident of their spiritual maturity, believing they could eat meat offered to idols and attend idol festivals without being affected. They were unconcerned about others or themselves. In contrast to their overconfidence, Paul asserted that self-denial is essential (9:27). Sometimes it is necessary to deny oneself even legitimate activities, such as the athlete who denies himself his rights because he wants to win a race. When Paul saw himself as being in a race to win the prize of leading others to Christ and maturing the saints, he had to exercise self-control (vv. 19-27). The Christian who's effective in service is self-disciplined. He doesn't use his liberty if doing so would offend a brother or an unsaved friend or put himself on the brink of temptation.

Liberty or Lust?

You often hear people say, "I'm a free man; I'm mature enough to handle most anything. An occasional 'R'-rated movie doesn't bother me. I pick out the philosophy of it. I study the human-interest factor. I can handle it."

"I know those office parties sometimes get out of control, but I go, have a 7 Up, and sit in the corner. I can take it; I'm mature."

"I know it's a wild party, but that's all right. I can have a few drinks with the boys, and it doesn't bother me. A little exposure keeps you in touch. You've got to be where they are, or you can't win them to Christ."

Paul was implying that such activities might fit into a category you haven't considered. Maybe what you justify as liberty is really lust.

Chapter 10 is a perfect illustration of an entire nation that couldn't handle its liberty. The Israelites became castaways. Having stretched their liberty to the precipice of sin, they fell. Paul shows how they received God's blessing, possessed God's privileges, and yet *all* died in the wilderness, useless to God and disqualified from service. And God took a new generation into the Promised Land.

Lesson

I. THE ASSETS OF LIBERTY (vv. 1-4)

A. Being Liberated by God's Power (v. 1)

"Moreover, brethren, I would not that ye should be ignorant, that all our fathers were under the cloud, and all passed through the sea."

Paul began by discussing the privileges Israel enjoyed because they parallel what the Christian enjoys. "Moreover" is a translation of the Greek word *gar,* a transitional word that demonstrates that 1 Corinthians 10:1-13 is based on the idea of being disqualified (9:27). "I would not that ye should be ignorant" underscores the importance of the Corinthians' understanding what he was about to say.

1. Domination

When did Israel pass through the sea and under the cloud? During the Exodus. For four hundred years Israel had been in Egypt without a national identity. They were in abject slavery, and from that platform there was no hope that they would ever be a witness to the world.

2. Deliverance

Finally God decided He would free them to establish them as a witnessing community. He parted the Red Sea and led them with His cloud. The cloud and the sea symbolized Israel's liberation from bondage—the touchstone of Judaism. When a Jewish person wants to demonstrate that Israel is God's elect people, he points back to the Exodus, for that was when God gave them an independent identity.

God's People

When Paul refers to the people of Israel as "our fathers," he is saying that they are our fathers in the sense of faith. Those of us who are Gentile believers are not the racial descendants of Abraham, but Galatians 3:29 says we are his seed by faith. Those who by faith lived as God's people are our *spiritual* forefathers, although that doesn't mean we are Jewish.

3. Designation

God freed his people from Egypt so that they might be a national witness. Their deliverance is not a picture of salvation. The nation was not saved by walking through the Red Sea. Rather, individuals were saved by believing God. Some Israelites were saved while still in Egypt. For example, Moses was a true believer before He led them out of Egypt. Later some were regenerated while Israel wandered in the wilderness, and some after they arrived in the Promised Land.

The Exodus was not an act of universal salvation; it was God's calling out a witnessing community. God chose a people who were subjugated, unable to set a pattern of godliness for the world. He delivered them and established them as His own independent community so that the world might observe what the people of God are like.

Like Israel, God has called the church to be His witnessing community. We have been freed from bondage and placed in the world to communicate His truth. But we must be cautious to avoid Israel's end: many died in the wilderness because their sin disqualified them. That doesn't mean those who were saved lost their salvation; it was that the nation became useless to God as a witness.

Israel was chosen to receive and preserve the Word of God and to prepare for the Messiah's coming. But one must remember that not all racial Israel is true Israel by faith. Paul said, "They are not all Israel, who are of Israel" (Rom. 9:6). Each Israelite, whether he exercised personal faith or not, had the marvelous privilege of being a part of God's witnessing nation.

4. Disqualification

A common mistake is to relate the death of the Israelites in the wilderness to salvation. Claiming that leaving

Egypt is synonymous with salvation, some interpreters say that those who died lost their salvation. Actually, this incident teaches that all the people, some of whom believed and some of whom did not, were disqualified from the witnessing community because they were unfaithful and fell into sin.

B. Being Labeled as God's People (v. 2)

"And were all baptized unto Moses in the cloud and in the sea."

1. The rite

a) Confusion

Immediately when you see the word *baptized* you probably think of sprinkling, immersing, or pouring. To get past the symbol to the reality of what the text is saying is difficult for us.

b) Clarification

Baptists may say that "were all baptized" refers to physical immersion when Israel went through the sea. Presbyterians may say that as Israel was under the cloud, it rained, and they were sprinkled. But neither can be correct. The Israelites couldn't have been immersed because they walked through on dry land, and it couldn't have rained because the Shekinah cloud was not full of water but of God's presence. Paul is not talking about physical baptism.

2. The reality

a) The symbolism examined

To the Christian, baptism signifies identification. When you believed in Jesus Christ, you were baptized into Him—associated or identified with Him. First Corinthians 6:17 says, "He that is joined unto the Lord is one spirit." Water baptism is the symbol of that identification. Because all believers are baptized into Christ, we are one not only with Him but also with each other. We are identified together in a corporate community under Christ's leadership.

b) The significance explained

Notice verse 1: "*all* . . . were under the cloud, and *all* passed through the sea"; verse 2: "were *all* baptized"; verse 3: "did *all* eat"; and verse 4: "did *all* drink" (emphasis added). By using "all" five times in the first four verses, Paul emphasizes that Israel was together in a corporate community under the leadership of Moses. They *all* identified with Moses. They *all* followed his leadership. As baptism brings us under the leadership of Christ, participation in the great events of the Exodus brought them under Moses. God liberated them and then made them His witnessing community. It's like God's calling the Christian to serve with other believers as the witnessing community of this age.

C. Being Showered with God's Provision (vv. 3-4)

1. The source (v. 3)

"And did all eat the same spiritual food."

"Spiritual" does not describe the essence of the food but its source. Spiritual food is provided by the Spirit of God. When the Israelites were in the wilderness, the Holy Spirit gave them manna to eat.

2. The sustenance (vv.3-4*a*)

"And did all eat the same spiritual food; and did all drink the same spiritual drink."

God always provided for their needs as he does for ours. We are supplied by Him (Phil. 4:19). John 6:35 says, "He that cometh to me shall never hunger, and he that believeth on me shall never thirst." We are sustained. "Eat" and "drink" are in the imperfect tense in the Greek text, which means they know no completion. The imperfect tense stresses continual action—"they were continually being fed." Throughout their wandering, throughout their lives, they were sustained by God.

3. The Sustainer (v. 4*b-c*)

"For they drank of that spiritual Rock that followed them, and that Rock was Christ."

"That Rock was Christ" is a thrilling statement because it proves the pre-incarnate existence of Jesus Christ—He followed Israel through the wilderness. By referring to Christ as the Rock, a title the Old Testament often uses for God, Paul was saying that Christ is equal to God.

In Exodus 17 God commands Moses to take his rod and strike a rock. Moses did, and it gushed out water and satisfied the thirst of a million or more people. According to Jewish legend, that rock followed Israel for the rest of the forty years, always yielding its water. I believe that Paul is alluding to that popular legend, but instead of using *petros,* the Greek word for boulder, he uses *petra,* which means "a massive cliff." According to the legend, a rolling boulder supplied Israel's water, but actually they drank from the rocky cliff that followed them—Christ. It was actually the Messiah who sustained Israel in the wilderness.

Christ was identified with His people even before His incarnation. The Old Testament people didn't have the indwelling Spirit, but they had the sustaining presence of Christ. In Old Testament times He was often called "the Angel of the Lord" or "the Angel of Jehovah," but He was there, caring for His people, fulfilling their needs.

II. THE ABUSES OF LIBERTY (vv. 5-10)

A. Stated (v. 5)

"But with many of them God was not well pleased; for they were overthrown in the wilderness."

1. The extent

"With many of them" literally means "most of them." Of the generation that left Egypt only two, Joshua and Caleb, entered the Promised Land.

2. The explanation

The Greek word translated "overthrown" means "strewn everywhere." Their corpses were strewn across the desert. God refused to allow them to establish a witnessing community. They died, and a new generation entered Canaan. They had all the privileges but became smug and self-confident. They constantly complained and abused their liberty, and they were disqualified.

3. The examination

According to 2 Timothy 2:20, even in the church there are vessels unto honor and dishonor. God has to depend upon a minority of Christians to do His ministry because so many are disqualified. Many Christians, like Israel, start serving the Lord Jesus Christ, fall into temptation and sin, and are disqualified from serving Christ. They will be in heaven because they have been regenerated, but they have squandered their spiritual assets and are therefore useless to God.

First Corinthians 11 tells us that some Corinthian believers died because they stretched their liberty to its limits, faced overwhelming temptation, and fell into sin. The Corinthian corpses were evidence of disqualification from service because of sin.

B. Summarized (v. 6)

"Now these things were our examples, to the intent we should not lust after evil things, as they also lusted."

1. Loathing God's provision

The Greek word translated "examples" (*tupos*) refers to a model, a type, or a pattern. The wilderness generation is an example that "we should not lust after evil things, as they also lusted." Their liberty turned into lust. God was supplying all their needs, but Numbers 11:4 says, "The children of Israel also wept again, and said, Who shall give us flesh [meat] to eat?" They were tired of manna and said, "Our soul is dried away; there is nothing at all, besides this manna, before our eyes" (Num. 11:6).

When I was a boy, I stayed with some friends all summer. Every day we had soup and sandwiches for lunch. Now when I see those friends they say, "John, remember when you would say, 'Soup and sandwiches—all we ever have here is soup and sandwiches'?" Israel was saying, "All we ever get is manna."

2. Lusting for the past

Numbers 11:5 says, "We remember the fish which we did eat in Egypt freely; the cucumbers, and the melons, and the leeks, and the onions, and the garlic." Verse 34 reveals that God killed those who lusted after such things. When you take your liberty to its extremity, it's easy to look back at the old life and lust after it. When you extend your liberty to the thin edge between what is your right and what is sin, you will be tempted to return to what God redeemed you from. Let that be a perpetual warning against lusting for the forbidden objects of your life before Christ.

3. Learning from God's purification

Psalm 78:27 says, "He rained flesh also upon them like dust, and feathered fowls like the sand of the sea." Verses 30-33 continue, "But while their food was yet in their mouths, the wrath of God came upon them, and slew the fattest of them, and smote down the chosen men of Israel. For all this they sinned still, and believed not in his wondrous works. Therefore, their days did he consume in vanity, and their years in trouble."

They wanted meat, and He gave them all they wanted. Then He killed the mightiest of them to purge that attitude from the witnessing community. The abuse of liberty disqualifies from service to Christ and can lead to death. Beware of overconfidence.

Focusing on the Facts

1. What are gray areas? Give some examples (see p. 8).
2. What should determine whether we exercise our liberty in gray areas (see p. 8)?
3. Why did the Corinthians believe they were free to do what they wanted (see pp. 8-9)?
4. What was the Corinthians' basic problem? How does 1 Corinthians 10:12 support your answer (see p. 10)?
5. Explain how each of the biblical examples demonstrated overconfidence (see pp. 10-13).
6. Instead of overconfidence Paul calls for ______________ (see p. 13).
7. The Exodus was not an act of ______________ ______________. Explain the significance of that statement (see p. 15).
8. Explain Israel's responsibilities concerning the Word of God and the Messiah (see p. 15).
9. Explain why Israel's "baptism" could not have been water baptism (see p. 16).
10. What does baptism signify to the Christian? Explain (see pp. 16-17).
11. God liberated Israel and made them His ______________ ______________ (see p. 17).
12. What does 1 Corinthians 10:4 teach about the Person of Christ (see p. 18)?
13. What was the Jewish legend concerning the rock in Exodus 17? Explain how Paul's word choice points away from that (see p. 18).
14. Although the Old Testament believers did not have the indwelling Spirit, they did have ______________ (see p. 18).
15. What does Numbers 11:5 imply will happen when you stretch liberty to its limits (see p. 20)?
16. What two events can occur when a Christian abuses his liberty (see p. 21)?

Pondering the Principles

1. First Corinthians 8 teaches us that in the gray areas we have liberty. But chapters 9 and 10 remind us that there are limitations. List several questionable activities in which you are exercising your liberty. Then, for each activity, list the names of people who may be caused to sin by following your example, and list any temptations you might face because of it. Pray to the Lord, thanking Him for your freedom and seeking His wisdom to know if you should limit your liberty in any of those areas. Ask God to keep you from an overconfident spirit.

2. The Israelites enjoyed tremendous spiritual privileges, as 1 Corinthians 10 attests. List the benefits you enjoy because of your relationship with Christ. Take time each day this week to meditate on those benefits and to praise God for His matchless grace in bestowing them.

2
The Danger of Overconfidence—Part 2

Outline

Introduction
A. Christian Liberty Is Granted by God
B. Christian Liberty Is Received Through the Gospel
C. Christian Liberty Offers Many Freedoms
  1. Freedom from ceremonial law
  2. Freedom from the curse of the law
  3. Freedom from the fear of death
  4. Freedom from the condemnation of sin
  5. Freedom from the rules of men
  6. Freedom from Jewish ordinances
D. Christian Liberty Is Bestowed upon All Christians
E. Christian Liberty Is to Be Protected
  1. An exclamation
  2. An example
  3. An exception
F. Christian Liberty Can Be Violated
  1. By offending others
  2. By disqualifying yourself from Christian service
    a) Disregarding the rules
    b) Lacking self-control

Review
I. The Assets of Liberty (vv. 1-4)
II. The Abuses of Liberty (vv. 5-10)
  A. Stated (v. 5)
  B. Summarized (v. 6)

Lesson
  C. Specified (vv. 7-10)

1. Worshiping idols (v. 7)
   a) Continuing exposure
      (1) The scenario
      (2) The warning
   b) Syncretism
      (1) In Corinth
      (2) In Israel
         (*a*) A golden image
         (*b*) A pagan feast
         (*c*) A swift response
         (*d*) A direct application
2. Practicing immorality (v. 8)
   a) A characteristic response
   b) A close relationship
      (1) In Israel
      (2) In Corinth
         (*a*) Their attitude
         (*b*) Their activity
3. Testing God (v. 9)
   a) Bordering the limits of liberty
   b) Breaking the limits of God's patience
4. Harboring complaints (v. 10)
   a) The destroyer
   b) The discontentment
   c) The destruction

Conclusion

Introduction

The key to 1 Corinthians 10:1-13 is verse 12: "Wherefore, let him that thinketh he standeth take heed lest he fall." You're most apt to fall when you believe you're strong. The theme of the first twelve verses in chapter 10 is the danger of overconfidence. Although this theme has a distinct identity, it is also woven together with chapters 8-10 to make an important point concerning Christian liberty: the Christian should not become overconfident but should realize he must limit his liberty.

Although the New Testament teaches in detail about Christian liberty, let's consider the major points that identify it.

A. Christian Liberty Is Granted by God

God gives liberty to the believer. John 8:36 says, "The Son . . . shall make you free," indicating that Christ is the agent of freedom. Galatians 5:1 refers to "the liberty with which Christ hath made us free." Colossians 1:13 says that the Father "hath delivered us from the power of darkness, and translated us into the kingdom of his dear Son." Second Corinthians 3:17 says, "Where the Spirit of the Lord is, there is liberty." Christian liberty comes from the Trinity—from the Godhead.

B. Christian Liberty Is Received Through the Gospel

John 8:31-32 tells us Jesus said, "to those Jews who believed on him, If ye continue in my word, then are ye my disciples indeed; and ye shall know the truth, and the truth shall make you free." Verse 36 concludes, "If the Son, therefore, shall make you free, ye shall be free indeed." Christian freedom is granted by God when we receive Jesus Christ.

C. Christian Liberty Offers Many Freedoms

1. Freedom from ceremonial law

We no longer need to keep ceremonial laws. An internal guideline, the Holy Spirit, has replaced external rules and regulations. Romans 7:6 says, "Now we are delivered from the law."

2. Freedom from the curse of the law

People who break the law are cursed. But Christ became a curse for us that we might not be cursed or condemned. Galatians 3:13 says, "Christ hath redeemed us from the curse of the law, being made a curse for us; for it is written, Cursed is everyone that hangeth on a tree." We are free from having to pay the penalty for our sin.

3. Freedom from the fear of death

Hebrews 2:15 says that Christ delivered "them who, through fear of death, were all their lifetime subject to bondage." We may fear pain and disease but not death itself because it ushers us into the presence of God.

4. Freedom from the condemnation of sin

   Romans 6:7 says, "He that is dead is freed from sin." Paul means we are free from the condemnation of sin. Sin cannot require anything of us because its penalty has been paid.

5. Freedom from the rules of men

   In 1 Corinthians 9:19 Paul asserts that believers are "free from all men." He means we are free from man-made rules and traditions.

6. Freedom from Jewish ordinances

   Galatians 4:3 and Colossians 2:20 add that we are free from religious traditions (rabbinic or pagan) that supersede and stifle God's revelation.

We possess what Paul calls "the glorious liberty of the children of God" (Rom. 8:21).

D. Christian Liberty Is Bestowed upon All Christians

Christian liberty belongs to *all* believers. Some Christians are not freer than others. In Galatians 5:13 Paul says, "Brethren, ye have been called unto liberty," implying that all Christians are called with a view toward liberty.

E. Christian Liberty Is to Be Protected

1. An exclamation

   The New Testament teaches us not to surrender our liberty but to enjoy it. Galatians 5:1 says, "Stand fast, therefore, in the liberty with which Christ hath made us free, and be not entangled again with the yoke of bondage."

2. An example

Paul was continually hounded by the Judaizers. They wanted him to keep the Mosaic law, circumcise all Gentile believers, and make the Gentiles keep the ceremonies of Moses. Galatians 2:4 says that "false brethren . . . came in secretly to spy out our liberty which we have in Christ Jesus, that they might bring us into bondage." The Judaizers were spying out the Gentile Christians' liberty to find where they were abusing it so they could force them back into bondage. However, Paul was free from Jewish ceremonialism and wouldn't subscribe to it. In verse 5 he gives his reason: "That the truth of the gospel might continue with you." If you give up your liberty to ritual, form, or tradition, people will confuse that with the truth of the gospel. If you identify your Christianity by what you don't do, people will believe that's what Christianity is.

3. An exception

Nevertheless, when Paul went to Jerusalem, he took a Jewish vow, which was part of the ceremonial law (Acts 21:17-26). In that instance he gave up his liberty to reach people for Christ. When the Judaizers harassed Paul to circumcise Gentile believers in Christ, he refused because the Gentiles didn't believe in circumcision. But he circumcised Timothy—whose father was a Gentile—so that his work among the Jews would be more effective (Acts 16:1-3). A Christian should never surrender his liberty needlessly, or people will confuse the gospel with what he does or doesn't do. He should, however, relinquish his liberty when exercising it might offend someone. Paul was willing to be a Jew to the Jews to win them, but he wouldn't turn Gentiles into Jews to appease the Jews.

F. Christian Liberty Can Be Violated

1. By offending others

What may be offensive varies from culture to culture and from year to year. Paul explains in chapter 9 that to offend others is to abuse your liberty. Recently I talked with a missionary who was in Europe. He and his companions were in a village where the women do not shave their legs. Only one type of woman there shaves her legs—a prostitute. When the missionary women arrived with shaved legs, problems arose. The missionary ladies had to relinquish their liberty to avoid offending and confusing those they were trying to reach. You abuse your liberty when you needlessly harm someone else.

2. By disqualifying yourself from Christian service

   A little boy climbed into a bunk bed one night, and in the middle of the night he fell out and hit the floor with a tremendous crash. His father came running, saw he was crying on the floor, and asked what happened. The boy responded, "I think I fell asleep too close to where I got in!" Many Christians have done the same thing. They flirt on the borderline, placing themselves in a position to fall into sin and be disqualified from service for Christ. Using Israel as an example, Paul illustrates that scenario in chapter 10.

   a) Disregarding the rules

   Paul's discussion in chapter 10 develops out of his comments in verses 24-27 of chapter 9 that we're all in a race to win people to Christ. But Paul understood that he must run according to the rules or be disqualified from the race. To be disqualified doesn't mean one loses his salvation; it means one ceases being useful in Christian service.

   b) Lacking self-control

   For Paul to serve effectively he had to bring his body into subjection, or be self-controlled (v. 27). He couldn't let his body do whatever it wanted, or he might sin and disqualify himself from the ministry. But that is exactly what happened to the Israelites. Because they refused to limit their liberty and control their bodies, they became disqualified. Commentator John Davis believes there may have been as many as two million participants in the Exodus (*Moses and the*

Gods of Egypt [Grand Rapids: Baker, 1971], p. 283). If two million left Egypt, that's how many died in the wilderness, excluding Joshua and Caleb.

Review

I. THE ASSETS OF LIBERTY (vv. 1-4; see pp. 14-18)

II. THE ABUSES OF LIBERTY (vv. 5-10; see pp. 18-21)

A. Stated (v. 5; see pp. 18-19)

B. Summarized (v. 6; see pp. 19-21)

Lesson

C. Specified (vv. 7-10)

1. Worshiping idols (v. 7)

"Neither be ye idolaters, as were some of them; as it is written, The people sat down to eat and drink, and rose up to play."

a) Continuing exposure

(1) The scenario

The Corinthians lived in a society in which idolatry permeated everything. The Corinthian Christians, smug and confident of their maturity, believed they could participate in social gatherings characterized by idolatry and remain unaffected. After all, they had been Paul's students for eighteen months (Acts 18:11). If their involvement consisted only of eating meat offered to idols, they assumed they could resist the temptation to participate further. Perhaps they believed that if an orgy began, they could sit in a corner and content themselves discussing theology. They thought they wouldn't become involved, and everywhere they went they exposed themselves to idolatry.

(2) The warning

Paul pointed the Corinthians to Israel. The Israelites were in the desert, where there weren't any idols, but the first time Moses was gone they reverted to Egyptian idolatry. The Corinthians were in a more precarious position because they lived in the middle of idolatry. By continually exposing themselves to it, they were becoming part of it.

Our Changing Morality

The morality of Christianity and society has changed dramatically. Fifty years ago social morality was much more confined to Scripture, but now even the morality of professing Christians is dissipating. Western society has sought to destroy all morality, and we have followed its lead. Constant exposure to society's values through the media has changed the church's morals.

b) Syncretism

When a professing believer flirts with idolatry, the result will be syncretism, a wedding between idolatry and true worship.

(1) In Corinth

Some Corinthian Christians had already wedded Christianity to idol worship. In 1 Corinthians 5:11 Paul says, "I have written unto you not to keep company, if any man that is called a brother [anyone calling himself a Christian] be a fornicator [committing sexual sin], or covetous, or an idolater." Apparently some within the congregation were worshiping idols.

(2) In Israel

In 1 Corinthians 10:7 Paul refers to an incident that is recorded in Exodus 32.

(*a*) A golden image

Exodus 32:1-4 says, "When the people saw that Moses delayed to come down out of the mount, the people gathered themselves together unto Aaron, and said unto him, Up, make us gods [Heb., *Elohim,* is the usual word for "God" and probably should be translated "God" here] which shall go before us; for as for this Moses, the man who brought us up out of the land of Egypt, we know not what is become of him. And Aaron said unto them, Break off the golden earrings, which are in the ears of your wives, of your sons, and of your daughters, and bring them unto me [perhaps an attempt to stop them by demanding that they supply the gold]. And all the people broke off the golden earrings which were in their ears, and brought them unto Aaron. And he received them at their hand, and fashioned it with an engraving tool, after he had made it a melted calf [an Egyptian deity]."

(*b*) A pagan feast

Exodus 32:5-6 tells us that "when Aaron saw it, he built an altar before it; and Aaron made proclamation, and said, Tomorrow is a feast to the Lord [Jehovah]. And they rose up early on the next day and offered burnt offerings, and brought peace offerings [traditional offerings to Jehovah]; and the people sat down to eat and to drink and rose up to play."

Knowing that Jehovah had freed them, they said the calf represented the God that brought them out of Egypt. The calf was an idol of Jehovah! That is religious syncretism. Israel translated the worship of the true God into paganism. For four hundred years they were exposed to Egyptian idolatry, and it had made its mark. Without Moses they immediately reverted to idolatry, connecting the true God with it. It is impossible to continually expose yourself to idolatry and not have it interfere with your theology. The Israelites celebrated a feast to Jehovah as they would a pagan feast. Verse 6 says they "sat down to eat and to drink, and rose up to play." The Hebrew word translated "play" is used in Genesis 26:8 where "Isaac was caressing Rebekah, his wife," which means he had sexual relations with her. They ate, got drunk, and then had an orgy—while claiming to worship God! When Moses came down from the mountain, the people were naked, engaging in revelry (v. 25).

(*c*) A swift response

Exodus 32:28 says, "And there fell of the people that day about three thousand men." Although God slew only three thousand immediately, the entire nation bore the guilt, and they all eventually died in the wilderness. God's liberated people fell because they never let go of Egypt.

(*d*) A direct application

The Corinthians had never let go of the old life. In 1 Corinthians 10:20 Paul says, "I say that the things which the Gentiles sacrifice, they sacrifice to demons, and not to God." Someone may have argued that their pagan sacrifices were being offered to the true God. Correcting them, Paul said idolaters are in fact sacrificing to demons. He continued, "I would not that ye should have fellowship with demons. Ye cannot drink the cup of the Lord, and the cup of demons; ye cannot be partakers of the Lord's table and of the table of demons" (vv. 20-21). They would partake of the Lord's Table and then go to an idolatrous feast. They had liberty in Christ to do those things, but Paul warned them if they abused their liberty, they—like Israel—would become engulfed in idolatry and disqualified from service.

An idolater doesn't have to worship a piece of wood or stone. In our society we have made idols of money, education, position, sex, sports, clothes, cars, and many other things. God said to the prophet Ezekiel, "Son of man, these men have set up their idols in their heart" (Ezek. 14:3-4; cf. v. 5). Idolatry is worshiping anything other than the true God.

Modern Idolatry

A minister I knew enjoyed golf and played several times a week. I thought he shouldn't play so often because he might become addicted, but he continued to play and later began to gamble. He lost small amounts at first, but finally he began losing between five hundred and three thousand dollars a game. He was forced to leave the ministry in disgrace because he had erected an idol and refused to surrender it. He had the freedom to play golf, but he allowed it to become a god. The Israelites fell because of an idol, the Corinthians were falling, and we will also fall if we have idols.

2. Practicing immorality (v. 8)

"Neither let us commit fornication, as some of them committed, and fell in one day three and twenty thousand."

Paul reminded his readers of what happened to Israel, recorded in Numbers 25.

a) A characteristic response

Someone may wonder about God's attitude toward sexual sin. His attitude is best expressed in this: when the Israelites engaged in idolatry and illicit sex with the Moabites, God killed twenty-three thousand of them in one day.

b) A close relationship

(1) In Israel

Numbers 25:1-3 says, "The people began to commit harlotry [sexual sin] with the daughters of Moab. And they called the people unto the sacrifices of their gods; and the people did eat, and bowed down to their gods. And Israel joined himself unto Baal-peor [the god Baal, a local deity, who was associated with Mount Peor]; and the anger of the Lord was kindled against Israel." Idolatry and sex have always been closely related.

(2) In Corinth

(*a*) Their attitude

The principal temple in Corinth was the temple of Venus, which was run by prostitutes and known for its orgies. The Corinthian believers wanted to attend the feasts held there and ignore the orgies. Paul reminded them that because the Israelites didn't divorce themselves from sexual immorality, twenty-three thousand of them died in one day.

How Many Died in Numbers 25?

Numbers 25:9 says twenty-four thousand died because of sexual immorality with Moab, but in 1 Corinthians 10:8 Paul says twenty-three thousand died—an apparent contradiction. There are several possible explanations.

1. A copyist's error

Discrepancies between a number cited in one passage and one cited in another could be a copyist's error. That any such variation is so minute emphasizes the remarkable accuracy of Scripture.

2. A round number

The writers may be using round numbers as Hebrew scribes often did. If the number that died was between twenty-three and twenty-four thousand, one writer may have rounded down to twenty-three, the other up to twenty-four.

3. A different reckoning

The writer of Numbers records a *total* of twenty-four thousand died, but Paul said twenty-three thousand died "in one day," leaving the possibility that a thousand more died on the second day. Therefore both could be correct.

(*b*) Their activity

The Corinthians already were attending immoral celebrations and reaping the consequences. One man was having sex with his father's wife, which may have begun at an idol feast (1 Cor. 5:1). In 1 Corinthians 6:18 Paul says, "Flee fornication [sexual immorality]." The implication is they were already participating (cf. 6:15-16). Some Corinthian believers had already died because of sin (11:30). While flaunting their freedom by idol worship, they had fallen into sexual sin.

Common Preludes to Sexual Sin

Sexual sin is still one of Satan's most effective traps. Young people often believe they are in control of everything. They believe that because they're Christians they can stir up sexual desires and then start quoting Bible verses! Married businessmen sometimes believe they won't be tempted by eating lunch or dinner with women at the office. Pastors may be confident that counseling women won't cause any problems. I know of a pastor who lost his ministry because he had sexual relationships with dozens of women he had counseled. Don't push your freedom too far. Many Christians are out of the race to win people to Christ because they exposed themselves to sexual temptation.

3. Testing God (v. 9)

"Neither let us put Christ to the test, as some of them also tested him, and were destroyed by serpents."

Speaking of the same incident, the book of Numbers says, "The people spoke against God, and against Moses, Wherefore have ye brought us up out of Egypt to die in the wilderness? For there is no bread, neither is there any water; and our soul loatheth this light bread [manna]. And the Lord sent fiery serpents among the people, and they bit the people; and many people of Israel died" (21:5-6).

a) Bordering the limits of liberty

The Israelites pushed to see how far God would go, saying, "We don't like what you're giving us. We want this, and we want that." Some Christians push God to the limit all the time. Their view of the Christian life is not, "How can I please God?" but, "How far can I go and get away with it?"

Peter said to Sapphira, who attempted to tell the same lie her husband had: "How is it that ye have agreed together to test the Spirit of the Lord? Behold, the feet of them who have buried thy husband are at the door, and shall carry thee out" (Acts 5:9). Both of them died as a result of their hypocrisy.

Satan tempted Christ by saying, "If thou be the Son of God, cast thyself down from here [the pinnacle of the temple]; for it is written, He shall give his angels charge over thee, to keep thee . . . lest at any time thou dash thy foot against a stone" (Luke 4:9-11). Christ responded, "Thou shalt not put the Lord, thy God, to the test" (v. 12). Don't place yourself in a situation and then attempt to force God to bring you out of it.

The Corinthians felt restricted with their new life in Christ. Pushing to the edge of their liberty, they demanded to have what they once enjoyed. They weren't willing to leave the old life and accept the new.

b) Breaking the limits of God's patience

The Corinthians decided to do what they used to do, expecting God to forgive them because of His grace. Paul reminded them of what happened to Israel when they pushed God's grace and patience too far. One day God decided to send poisonous snakes to their camp, and many people died.

That was something for the Corinthians to consider because some in their congregation had already died or were sick because they pushed God too far by partaking of Communion with sin in their lives (11:30). God is gracious, but He will not tolerate sin.

4. Harboring complaints (v. 10)

"Neither murmur ye, as some of them also murmured, and were destroyed by the destroyer."

a) The destroyer

The destroyer is the angel of death who slew the first-born in Egypt (Ex. 12:23), the Israelites following David's census (2 Sam. 24:16), and the Assyrians who went up against Judah (2 Chron. 32:21). God used that angel to slay those who murmured in the wilderness.

b) The discontentment

The Corinthians were discontent with God's putting any restrictions on their life-styles. Their murmuring showed dissatisfaction with God's will for them. They hadn't learned to say with Paul, "I have learned, in whatever state I am, in this to be content" (Phil. 4:11). Unfortunately, many Christians tend to complain about where they live, whom they're married to, what their financial condition is, where they work, and what tragedies in life they encounter. When you complain about what God has chosen for your life, you're murmuring.

c) The destruction

In Numbers 16, the passage Paul alludes to in verse 10, Korah and his companions expressed dissatisfaction with their circumstances and rebelled against Moses' leadership. God killed many of the rebels (vv. 31-35). When the people complained about that the next day, God sent a plague that consumed 14,700 of them (vv. 41-49).

Conclusion

Paul warned the Corinthians that a lack of self-control will lead to abuse of liberty through idolatry, sexual sin, tempting God, and complaining. Continually playing with questionable matters reveals a lack of self-control and should warn us that we may be abusing our liberty. In 1 Corinthians 10:11 Paul says, "Now all these things happened unto them [the Israelites] for examples, and they are written for our admonition [instruction], upon whom the ends of the ages are come." We are the last dispensation (the last days of world history before the messianic kingdom comes) and should learn from what happened to Israel so we don't fall into the same traps and become disqualified. May God help us to be useful to Him as a witnessing community. As you enjoy your liberty, always remember two things: don't abuse your liberty by offending others or by living so close to the edge that you fall.

Focusing on the Facts

1. Explain the major points that the New Testament makes about Christian liberty (see pp. 25-29).
2. Our freedom is defined as freedom from what (see pp. 25-26)?
3. What does Galatians 5:1 teach about liberty (see p. 26)?
4. Why is it important not to give up your liberty to ritual (see p. 27)?
5. Explain why Paul kept the ceremonial law by taking a Jewish vow (see p. 27).
6. What does it mean to be disqualified (see p. 28)?
7. When a professing believer flirts with idolatry, the result will be ________________. Explain (see p. 30).

8. Whom did the golden calf represent? Explain (see p. 31).
9. Is idolatry limited to worshiping objects made of wood or stone? Explain (see p. 33).
10. ________________ and ________________ have always been closely related (see p. 34).
11. What are the possible solutions to the discrepancy between Numbers 25:9 and 1 Corinthians 10:8 (see pp. 34-35)?
12. Explain the consequences of the Corinthians' attending local pagan celebrations (see p. 35).
13. How were the Corinthians tempting God (see p. 36)?
14. What is murmuring? Give some examples (see p. 37).
15. What is a warning sign that we may be abusing our liberty (see p. 38)?

Pondering the Principles

1. Romans 8:21 speaks of "the glorious liberty of the children of God." To enjoy it fully requires that you understand the liberties you have. Re-read what you have been freed from (pp. 25-26). Meditate on how each aspect affects you and thank the Lord for your liberty. Have you allowed anyone to make you captive to the rules or traditions of men? Determine to make God's Word your only authority.

2. Idolatry is not only worshiping wood and stone images but also entertaining false or low thoughts about the true God. Do you have any misconceptions about God? Realize that they demean His character. The most important thing about you is what you conceive God to be because you will act toward Him according to what you believe He is like. Read through 1 John, noting every statement John makes about the Persons of the Trinity (e.g., noting that 1 John 1:5 says that God is light). Also notice any verbs that have God as the subject that might reveal something about Him (e.g., noting that 1 John 1:9 says that God forgives us). Keep a journal record of your findings. After you finish 1 John, continue your journal in your daily Bible study, taking time each day to praise God for His character.

3
The Danger of Overconfidence—Part 3

Outline

Introduction
- A. Illustrations of Temptation
  1. Christ
  2. Job
  3. Abraham
- B. Information About Temptation
  1. Its source
  2. Its purpose

Review
- I. The Assets of Liberty (vv. 1-4)
- II. The Abuses of Liberty (vv. 5-10)

Lesson
- III. The Application Regarding Liberty (vv. 11-13)
  - A. The Purpose (v. 11)
    1. Israel is an example (v. 11*a*)
    2. Israel is a warning (v. 11*b*)
  - B. The Principle (v. 12)
  - C. The Postscript (v. 13)
    1. The temptation of man (v. 13*a-b*)
       - *a*) Its course (v. 13*a*)
         - (1) The external circumstances
         - (2) Our internal response
       - *b*) Its commonness (v. 13*a-b*)
         - (1) No superhuman exceptions
         - (2) No satisfactory excuses

2. The faithfulness of God (v. 13*c-e*)
    a) Declared (v. 13*c*)
        (1) Deuteronomy 7:9
        (2) Lamentations 3:23
        (3) Psalm 36:5
        (4) 1 Corinthians 1:9
        (5) Job 5:19
    b) Demonstrated (v. 13*d-e*)
        (1) The way of escape presented
        (2) The way of escape practiced
            (*a*) Pray to the Lord
            (*b*) Trust in the Lord
            (*c*) Focus on Christ

Conclusion

Introduction

The key word in verse 13 is "temptation" (Gk., *peirasmos*). The English word *temptation* connotes seduction to sin. However, the Greek word translated "temptation" has no moral connotation. *Peirasmos* isn't necessarily good or evil but is a neutral word, meaning "to test," "to try," or "to prove."

A. Illustrations of Temptation

1. Christ

Matthew 4:1 says that Jesus was "led up of the Holy Spirit into the wilderness to be tempted of the devil" (KJV). If the word translated "tempted" meant "to seduce to sin" then that means the Holy Spirit attempted to seduce Jesus! Actually, the Holy Spirit led Jesus into the wilderness to be tested, not intending it to be a solicitation to evil but to good. Having revealed His righteousness, the tests would give confidence to Him and to the rest of the world at the beginning of His ministry that He would not sin. Although the Holy Spirit used Satan, He did not want to seduce Christ to evil but to prove His righteousness. The Holy Spirit tests us to bring us to righteousness, but Satan desires to turn those tests into temptations to sin.

2. Job

God didn't allow Satan to test Job in order to make him sin but to prove him righteous (Job 1:8). Sometimes God will allow Satan to intervene in our lives, but His design is always that we would respond righteously, not that we would be seduced into evil.

3. Abraham

In the King James Version, Hebrews 11:17 seems to imply that God tempted Abraham. But God didn't try to make Abraham do something evil; by asking him to sacrifice his son Isaac, God tested Abraham to see if he trusted Him and would obey at any cost (Gen. 22).

B. Information About Temptation

The noun *peirasmos* and the verb *peirazō* derive their meaning from the context. If the context is negative, the meaning is "to tempt to sin." If the context is positive—as God's testing of Abraham—the meaning is "to test for the purpose of strengthening righteousness." The context reveals the source and purpose of *peirasmos,* which determine its meaning.

1. Its source

James 1:13-14 says, "Let no man say when he is tempted, I am tempted of God; for God cannot be tempted with evil, neither tempteth he any man; but every man is tempted [to do evil] when he is drawn away of his own lust, and enticed." God tests us, but He never tempts us. Temptation to evil comes from the lust generated by our fallen, sinful flesh, not from God. Although Hebrews could imply that God tempted Abraham, and James says God tempts no man, there is no contradiction, just two different uses of a neutral term. God solicited Abraham to do good; lust solicits us to do evil. The word can have a good or bad source and, consequently, a good or bad connotation.

2. Its purpose

James said, "My brethren, count it all joy when ye fall into divers temptations; knowing this, that the trying of your faith worketh patience. But let patience have her perfect work" (James 1:2-4, KJV). Here we see that some temptations have perfection as their purpose, whereas others can lead to sin and disobedience (vv. 13-14). God tests with the goal of righteousness; Satan tempts with the goal of unrighteousness.

John 6:6 says that Christ put His disciple Philip to the test. In that context "test" is obviously not a solicitation to evil. In 2 Corinthians 13:5 Paul says, "Examine [*peirazō*] yourselves, whether you are in the faith; prove yourselves." The Corinthians were to prove themselves as Christians.

In Scripture the word *temptation* is neutral and can be translated "try," "test," "prove," "assay," or "tempt." It obtains its moral value from the context by determining who is testing and why.

Review

Because they had been delivered from Judaistic ceremonialism and pagan religion, the Corinthians were enjoying their new freedom in Christ. They were no longer captive to the curse of the law, fear of death, or sin's dominion. And they relished what Paul called "the glorious liberty of the children of God" (Rom. 8:21) by extending it to its limits. Paul wrote 1 Corinthians 8-10 to remind them that when they exercised their liberty in non-moral areas they were to remember the principles that limited it.

First, we must avoid offending people. If my liberty offends someone, it is wrong. That's Paul's subject in chapter 9. Using himself as an illustration, he reminded the believers in Corinth that he had a right to receive financial support from them, but he refused to exercise that right, fearing he might offend someone. We should be willing to limit our liberty out of love for others.

Another reason for limiting our liberty is to avoid disqualifying ourselves from Christian service. Christians who are concerned only about their freedom tend to stretch it to its limits. But if one continually flirts at the edges of the system, running his liberty out as far as possible, he is liable to fall into sin and be disqualified from usefulness.

I. THE ASSETS OF LIBERTY (vv. 1-4; see pp. 14-18)

Chapter 10 illustrates the second limitation. Israel had received numerous spiritual privileges from God. They had been freed from bondage in Egypt and were traveling toward the Promised Land.

II. THE ABUSES OF LIBERTY (vv. 5-10; see pp. 18-38)

But Israel lived too close to the edge of their liberty and fell into sin. Verses 7-10 catalog their sins of idolatry, immorality, testing God, and complaining. Because of those sins as many as two million people died in the wilderness disqualified. God couldn't use them as His witnessing nation because of their sin.

Paul wanted the Corinthians to know that although the Bible doesn't expressly forbid attending as opposed to participating in pagan festivals, they couldn't continually expose themselves to idolatry and immorality without eventually being drawn into sin. Having stated the illustration, he applied it.

Lesson

III. THE APPLICATION REGARDING LIBERTY (vv. 11-13)

A. The Purpose (v. 11)

1. Israel is an example (v. 11*a*)

"Now all these things happened unto them for examples."

Everything that happened to Israel is an example to us. Like Israel, we are free. We are God's witnessing community under the leadership of Christ. And God is our guide and provider. But as we enjoy the same blessings and privileges they enjoyed, we can misuse our liberty and fall into sin. We have to temper our freedom with self-control and remain within liberty's limits.

2. Israel is a warning (v. 11*b*)

"They are written for our admonition, upon whom the ends of the ages are come."

"Admonition" comes from the verb *noutheteō,* which speaks of counseling someone to change his behavior in light of imminent judgment. You're admonishing when you warn someone to change his way or expect trouble. Paul used Israel as an illustration to warn the Corinthians to change. The phrase "the ends of the ages" refers to the last dispensation. What happened to Israel is a warning to the Corinthians—and to all of us who live in this last age before Christ comes—that one can be part of the witnessing community yet forfeit his usefulness to God by abusing his liberty.

B. The Principle (v. 12)

"Wherefore, let him that thinketh he standeth take heed lest he fall."

Paul summarizes the previous eleven verses with one timeless principle: when someone believes he stands firm—like the smug Corinthians who believed they could misuse their liberty and not be hurt—he's about to fall. Proverbs 16:18 says, "Pride goeth before destruction, and an haughty spirit before a fall." Like Israel and Corinth, we are called to be a witnessing community. But when anyone becomes self-confident because he's a member of the witnessing community and has knowledge of the Bible and theological prowess, he's in danger of falling. Christians are most vulnerable when they believe they're secure, because they tend to stop leaning on the Lord and lean on their own insufficient resources.

C. The Postscript (v. 13)

"There hath no temptation taken you but such as is common to man; but God is faithful, who will not permit you to be tempted above that ye are able, but will, with the temptation, also make the way to escape, that ye may be able to bear it."

Paul closes the paragraph with a postscript that at first glance may seem disconnected, but he has a direct purpose in mind. He has told the Corinthians to avoid temptation by limiting their liberty, yet even if they were to limit themselves, they couldn't always avoid temptation. What should they do when tempted? Paul writes verse 13 not only to comfort them with God's faithfulness but also to inform them that if they sin, they can't blame their circumstances. That's because they'd never face a temptation they couldn't escape. But if they didn't escape, the fault would be theirs because here we learn that God always provides the way out.

1. The temptation of man (v. 13*a-b*)

a) Its course (v. 13*a*)

"There hath no temptation taken you."

(1) The external circumstances

God brings external circumstances into our lives as tests. James 1:2 says, "Count it all joy when ye fall into various trials." The Greek verb translated "fall into" (*peripiptō*) reminds us that circumstances that try us are outside us, not inside. For example, think of the balloon payment on the house or a huge medical bill decimating one's resources. Job had a financial shortage; he lost everything. All his plans went awry. Then he became sick, which is another external test. We all suffer sometime from the the death of a friend or family member as Job did. Or perhaps you discover that your partner in a business deal is a crook, and you have to decide what to do. You might find yourself maligned maliciously and persecuted for your faith. Perhaps, like Joseph, who was tested continually by Potiphar's wife, you are in a place where people are always encouraging you to join their sin. All those are tests.

(2) Our internal response

When one internalizes an external test so that his lust is kindled, and he is enticed to do evil, the test has become a temptation. For example, suppose you have a financial shortage. Your first thought may be that it is an exciting time for the Lord to reveal Himself to you. Then, after dwelling on your circumstances you convince yourself that you could help the Lord and take a few illegitimate deductions on your income tax. Your test has become a temptation because instead of giving the test to the Lord, you internalized it, kindling your lust. Or, maybe your plans fall through, and your first response is to trust the Lord and to wait to see His plan. But you begin wondering why things had to happen the way they did and begin worrying about the future. You've allowed a test to become a temptation.

A test is an opportunity for us to grow, but it can easily change into a temptation—a solicitation to sin. Although temptation isn't sin, one can't go from trial to sin without going through temptation first. It is best to keep the tests external. God tests us to stretch our spiritual muscles, but if we internalize the tests, our lusts—not God—will turn them into a solicitation to do evil. James 1:14 says, "Every man is tempted, when he is drawn away of his own lusts, and enticed."

Does God Lead Us into Temptation?

One of the petitions in the Lord's Prayer is: "Lead us not into temptation" (Matt. 6:13). To ask God not to lead us into temptation assumes He will if we don't ask. But James 1:13 says God leads no one into evil, so the prayer can't be asking God not to tempt us with evil. However, it also can't be asking God not to test us to make us strong because we know that is His will. The petition can be paraphrased, "Lord, don't let my trial become a temptation, leading me into sin." The next statement, "But deliver us from evil [Gk., *tou ponērou*, "the evil one"]," is parallel and proves its meaning. We must ask the Lord to intervene and not allow a test to become an opportunity for Satan to hurt us.

Temptation occurs when Satan or our flesh twists a test into an internal solicitation to evil; the idea in the Christian life is to keep your tests as tests.

b) Its commonness (v. 13*a*-*b*)

"But such as is common to man [Gk., *anthrōpinos*, "human"]."

(1) No superhuman exceptions

The Corinthians may have concluded that their temptations were supernatural, but Paul said all temptations are *human*. Often people sin and refuse personal responsibility by blaming demons or the devil, as if they were totally helpless and were oppressed by a supernatural being. But no one will ever have a superhuman temptation; every temptation that confronts us is "common to man."

It is startling to note that the temptations of Jesus were never supernatural, only human. Hebrews 4:15 says Jesus "was in all points tempted like as we are, yet without sin." Since James 1:13 says "God cannot be tempted with evil," Christ could be tempted only in His humanness. Jesus had the same temptations you and I have. He is, therefore, a faithful high priest who "is able to help them that are tempted" (Heb. 2:18).

James said to "confess your sins to one another" (5:16, NASB*) because we share a common strug-

**New American Standard Bible.*

gle. Paul mentioned that we can bear one another's burdens because we know we have the same problems (Gal. 6:2). Sometimes people say, "I would never say what I've done. It might shock you." I respond, "Shock me? Have you done something no one else has ever done? Have you had a temptation no one else has ever had?" Every temptation is common to man—the lust of the flesh, the lust of the eyes, and the pride of life (1 John 2:16). The unity of believers within the Body allows us to pour out our hearts to each other, confess our sins to each other, and support each other because we're all the same.

Since temptations are human, and we have divine resources, we always have the ability to handle what comes our way. First John 4:4 says, "Greater is he that is in you, than he that is in the world." No one ever needs to feel overwhelmed.

(2) No satisfactory excuses

Another thought about the commonness of temptation is that you can't blame God. Temptation is inevitable because of our humanness, but because the temptation is common to man, we can't blame God, because He won't allow us to be tempted beyond human capacity.

2. The faithfulness of God (v. 13*c*-*e*)

a) Declared (v. 13*c*)

"But God is faithful."

That declaration, which means that God keeps His promises, is the great key to verse 13. God's faithfulness is loudly proclaimed throughout Scripture.

(1) Deuteronomy 7:9—"Know, therefore, that the Lord thy God, he is God, the faithful God, who keepeth covenant and mercy."

(2) Lamentations 3:23—"Great is thy faithfulness."

(3) Psalm 36:5—"Thy faithfulness reacheth unto the clouds."

(4) 1 Corinthians 1:9—"God is faithful" (cf. 1 Thess. 5:24).

(5) Job 5:19—"He shall deliver thee in six troubles; yea, in seven there shall no evil touch thee." To the Hebrew mind the number *seven* symbolized completion, because God ceased from His creative works on the seventh day of creation. God will take care of everything. He is faithful.

b) Demonstrated (v. 13*d*-*e*)

"Who will not permit you to be tempted above that ye are able, but will, with the temptation, also make *the* way to escape, that ye may be able to bear it" (italics added).

Because God is faithful, His promise not to permit us to be tempted beyond our ability is as certain as every other promise He has made. He said He loves us; He means it and will keep His word. He said He saved us and has prepared a place for us; He will keep His promise. He promised that we will never have a temptation we can't handle; He will honor that promise also. First Corinthians 10:13 is the answer to the prayer in Matthew 6:13, "Lead us not into temptation [i.e., help us to keep our trials from becoming temptations]." In verse 13 Paul says God will. God won't let us be tempted beyond our resources. We sin because we don't take advantage of those resources.

(1) The way of escape presented

The article before "way" is definite in the Greek text, making it read "the way to escape." When I was younger, I used a translation that read, "a way of escape." I used to think, *I wonder what the way out of this temptation is*—assuming each temptation had a different way out. But every test and every temptation has the *same* way out. The focus of the way out is what immediately follows: "That ye may be able to bear it." Testing is a tunnel, and the only way out is through. Endurance is the way of escape.

Often we pray, "O Lord, my friend's going through a trial. Lord, teach him what You want him to know. Take him through until he learns it and then deliver him." That's a good prayer. But when we have a test, we say, "Lord, get me out of this test *now*!" Yet there isn't a quick way out.

When Jesus was tempted by the devil, He didn't escape by leaving but by staying and bearing the full force of Satan's attacks. When you face a trial, realize at the beginning that it is a test from God, and the only way it can accomplish its perfect work in you is for you to go through it. The stem of the Greek verb translated "bear" means "to carry," and *hupo,* the preposition connected to it, means "under." It is similar to the Greek word translated "to endure" (*hupomenō,* "to remain under").

(2) The way of escape practiced

Since the way of escape is enduring tests and temptations, let's discover how we can endure. There are three keys.

(*a*) Pray to the Lord

Jesus said, "Watch ye and pray, lest ye enter into temptation" (Mark 14:38). Without prayer a test can become a temptation. The first thing you should do when you have a test is pray: "God, I'm defenseless. Don't let me get into a test I can't withstand. Father, deliver me from the evil one. I lean on You; I must have Your strength." To endure you have to pray.

(*b*) Trust in the Lord

Peter said to know "that the same afflictions are accomplished in your brethren that are in the world. But the God of all grace, who hath called us unto his eternal glory by Christ Jesus, after ye have suffered a while, make you perfect, establish, strengthen, settle you" (1 Peter 5:9-10). You have to trust that God has sent the trial into your life for a purpose. In verse 9 Peter says to resist the devil's attacks by being "steadfast in the faith." Faith in what? That God has a purpose in testing you. You can keep the test external by saying, "O God, I give You this trial and ask You to care for me in it. I trust Your purpose in testing me, and by Your grace I know I will come through it." That's the way out, and when you emerge from the test, you will be strengthened. If, however, you collapse under it, you waste any opportunity for growth.

(*c*) Focus on Christ

Hebrews 12:3-4 says to "consider him that endured such contradiction of sinners against himself, lest ye be wearied and faint in your minds. Ye have not yet resisted unto blood, striving against sin." Christ was able to endure trials and temptation. He endured Satan's constant attacks. I believe that because Christ never sinned, He experienced the worst possible trials, for He endured them all to their limits. Hebrews 12 tells us to remember Christ when we are tired of bearing up under the tests. After all we haven't "yet resisted unto blood." When you think you have difficulties, remember what He endured.

Conclusion

You're going to have tests, but don't let them become temptations. You can endure by praying, trusting God's purposes, leaning on Jesus Christ, and focusing on what He endured.

A great illustration of those principles is in John Bunyan's classic allegory *The Pilgrim's Progress*. Christian and Hopeful were on their way to the Celestial City, traveling down the King's Highway. But they were diverted and lay down to sleep in a field that belonged to Giant Despair, who lived in Doubting Castle. Giant Despair found Christian and Hopeful asleep and locked them into a slimy, smelly dungeon.

The giant didn't kill them but beat them so badly that they wanted to kill themselves. That's a great illustration of despair! Finally, Christian said to Hopeful, "What a fool am I, thus to lie in a stinking dungeon, when I may as well walk at liberty! I have a key in my bosom called Promise, that will, I am persuaded, open any lock in Doubting Castle" ([New York: Simon and Schuster, 1957], p. 114). Taking the key of promise, he unlocked the bars and the castle gate and walked out of Doubting Castle.

John Bunyan was saying that if we let our trials turn into temptations, we will end up in Doubting Castle under the lock of Giant Despair. But knowledge of God's promises will free us. God has promised that He is faithful, that He has a purpose, and that He will bring us through. First Corinthians 10:13 is our key of promise. God will never leave us alone and will provide the way of escape from any trial, which means through it. Those promises free us from doubt and despair.

When we abuse our liberty and our trials turn into temptations, we should remember that none of them is ever more than we can endure. If we fall, however, we are to blame. Let that be a comfort and a warning.

Focusing on the Facts

1. Explain the difference between the English word *temptation* and the Greek word *peirasmos* (see p. 42).

2. Why did the Holy Spirit test Christ (see p. 42)?
3. What determines the meaning of *peirasmos*? Explain (see pp. 43-44).
4. How is Israel an example to us (see pp. 45-46)?
5. What time period is "the ends of the ages" (see p. 46)?
6. Explain how verse 13 is related to verses 1-12 (see p. 47).
7. How does an external test become a temptation (see p. 48)?
8. What does "lead us not into temptation" mean (see pp. 48-49)?
9. What does "common to man" literally mean? What conclusions about temptation can one draw from that definition (see pp. 49-50)?
10. Explain the nature of Christ's temptation (see p. 49).
11. How does God's faithfulness express itself in action (see p. 51)?
12. How does the definite article affect the interpretation of "way of escape" (see pp. 51-52)?
13. What is *the* way of escape? Explain (see p. 52).
14. What are the keys to enduring temptation? Explain each (see pp. 52-53).

Pondering the Principles

1. The writer of Hebrews presents Christ as our great High Priest, who, having been one of us, can empathize with us. Read Hebrews 2:17-18 and 4:14-16, paying careful attention to what Jesus Christ has in common with us. How should knowing that change what we do and think in times of temptation? Memorize 2:18 and 4:16, taking time each morning this week to meditate on their meaning.

2. James 5:16 is a command: "Confess your sins to one another" (NASB). Galatians 6:2 is also a command: "Bear ye one another's burdens, and so fulfill the law of Christ." That first command we often neglect because of pride or fear of rejection, and the second one we often neglect because we don't want to become involved in others' lives. Too often our overall commitment to our Christian brothers and sisters grows weak. Using a concordance, look up all the New Testament references where "one another" appears. List each new command you discover about how we are to treat one another. Plan how to actively obey one of those commands today. Make it a lifetime practice to put the warmth of Christian love on display.

3. It is thrilling not only to know that God provides the way of escape from temptation but also that He provides it because He is faithful. He keeps His promises. Think of five biblical promises God has made to believers. Write down as many Scripture passages as you can think of that describes them, and study those passages. Take time now to thank Him for those precious promises and for His character, which binds Him to keep them.

4
The Truth About Idolatry

Outline

Introduction
- A. The Principle of Liberty
- B. The Debate Regarding Liberty
  1. The sphere
  2. The setting
  3. The schism
  4. The sensitivity
  5. The solution

Lesson
- I. The Godly Reaction to Idolatry (vv. 14-15)
  - A. A Simple Statement (v. 14)
  - B. A Reasonable Conclusion (v. 15)
- II. The General Range of Idolatry
  - A. Its Seriousness
  - B. Its Scope
    1. Slandering God's character
       - *a*) The explanation
       - *b*) The illustrations
         - (1) Abusing the name of Jesus
         - (2) Not trusting in God
    2. Worshiping the true God in a wrong way
    3. Worshiping any image
    4. Worshiping angels
    5. Worshiping devils
    6. Worshiping the dead

7. Being preoccupied with anything other than God
    a) Summarized
    b) Specified
        (1) Greed
        (2) Lust

III. The Grim Results of Idolatry
  A. It Defiles You
  B. It Pollutes Others
  C. It Doesn't Help
  D. It Brings Judgment
    1. Described in Ezekiel
    2. Described in Isaiah
  E. It Destroys Good Judgment

Conclusion

Introduction

First Corinthians deals with problems that faced the Corinthian assembly—and that face all believers. The Corinthians had many questions, one of which was whether they should eat meat that had been offered to idols. That introduced the question of Christian liberty in areas the Bible doesn't address. What are we free to do? What are the limits of our liberty?

A. The Principle of Liberty

From 1 Corinthians 8:1–11:1 Paul discusses that believers are no longer bound by ceremonies or traditions, ritual or form. We are free from religious trappings such as the observing of holy days, new moons, feasts, and sabbaths—free to be guided internally by the indwelling Holy Spirit.

B. The Debate Regarding Liberty

1. The sphere

Although the Bible forbids many things and encourages many others, some areas aren't even mentioned. The decisions we have to make usually involve knowing what is right to do in those areas. In what sphere is our liberty to operate? The Corinthians raised that issue by asking one question: Can we eat meat offered to an idol?

2. The setting

   In New Testament times pagans offered meat to various idols. The temple priests ate what they wanted and sold the rest to a local butcher, who would sell the meat at a lower price. If you went to someone's home, you might eat meat that had been offered to an idol. While shopping, you might even buy such meat to save money.

3. The schism

   Was it right to eat that meat? The mature Corinthians had decided it was, because they knew idols were nothing (1 Cor. 8:4). They knew God didn't care what they ate (Mark 7:19; 1 Tim. 4:4). But the newer Christians, who were weaker, argued that, having been saved out of idolatry, they couldn't eat it. Because the meat stirred vivid memories of their idolatry, they believed eating it would defile them. There was conflict in the assembly.

4. The sensitivity

   The Corinthians introduced an important point: although we might technically have liberty to do a certain thing, another consideration—how it will affect someone else—may restrict our liberty. We need to be sensitive. An activity may be allowed morally and scripturally, but we must consider how it will affect someone who hasn't yet matured to that level of understanding.

A Modern Gray Area

I remember a man who was saved while he was a rock musician. Consequently, he had nothing but hatred for rock music because of its association with drugs and immorality. Once he told me he believed that any music that sounds like rock is wrong and that a Christian should never listen to it. When I asked why he believed that, he answered, "Because I have such a hate for it." Although his answer was subjective, you can understand why he couldn't accept it. But maybe you were reared in a sheltered environment, have never been exposed to the ugly side of what you deem to be acceptable, and therefore arrive at a different conclusion. Music is just one example of a gray area, one of many in every culture and in every period of history.

5. The solution

Paul said there are two answers to their question. First, one must ask himself how his actions will affect others: Will he offend a weak Christian or an unbeliever? Second, he must consider how his actions might affect himself. If he indulges himself on the edge of sin, he might fall in. Many Corinthian Christians believed that eating meat offered to idols was not a problem, whether they bought it from the marketplace and ate it at home or whether they ate it at a friend's home. Moreover, they reasoned that they should become involved in their society, and, since every facet of it was connected to idolatry, they went to the temples and participated in the festivals. What they were really doing was pushing their liberty to its boundaries. That's why Paul advised them to limit their liberty based on how it affected others and how it affected themselves. The former he illustrates in chapter 9, the latter in chapter 10.

Lesson

I. THE GODLY REACTION TO IDOLATRY (vv. 14-15)

A. A Simple Statement (v. 14)

"My dearly beloved, flee from idolatry."

By going to the edge of the allowable, one can easily fall into sin. Those in Corinth who were convinced that an idol was nothing, and that what one ate didn't matter, were being induced to attend idolatrous temple feasts. And apparently some had fallen into sin, because 1 Corinthians 5:11

tells us that some calling themselves brothers were fornicators, drunkards, and idolaters. Perhaps those who attended the festivals didn't intend to worship or engage in idolatry. They came to eat the meal, enjoy their friends, and maintain their business contacts. But things got out of hand.

The thesis of Paul's discussion is this: the issue is not how near we can get to sin, but how far we can stay away. Rather than advocating that they run to the edge of idolatry, he told them to flee from it—to go the opposite direction. My Christian liberty doesn't permit me to expose myself needlessly to temptation and sin. I've often said that Christian liberty is not freedom to do wrong but freedom to do right for the first time in one's life.

"My dearly beloved" is the translation of an uncommon Greek phrase. It expresses Paul's deep concern for them. His words are not academic but emotional. Paul cared about these people. He said, "My dearly beloved, flee." He used the present imperative—"continually be fleeing from idolatry."

B. A Reasonable Conclusion (v. 15)

"I speak as to wise men; judge ye what I say."

"Wise men" (Gk., *phronimos*) is better translated "intelligent men." Intelligent men were to judge what Paul said. His argument is not obscure. The Corinthians were intelligent enough to understand his reasoning and to conclude that his logic was sound. He says to run from idolatry, and if they had thought it through, they would have agreed with him and obeyed.

II. THE GENERAL RANGE OF IDOLATRY

Let's examine the word *idolatry.* The term itself is repulsive. It fits in my vocabulary with words such as *blasphemy, damned, hell,* and *Judas.* It evokes great anxiety in me to protect the holiness, purity, and character of God.

A. Its Seriousness

I believe idolatry is one of the most serious and contaminating of sins, because it assaults the character of God. Once you adulterate His character, you lose the guidelines for every moral judgment. Unless one has a right perspective of God, everything is chaos. Thus the first three of the Ten Commandments confront idolatry.

B. Its Scope

Since idolatry is so heinous, and the Bible discusses it so often, we need to understand what it is.

1. Slandering God's character

a) The explanation

Idolatry libels God and slanders His character, reflecting the heart of sin and Satan. The idolatrous heart assumes that God is other than He is. A. W. Tozer said, "A God begotten in the shadows of a fallen heart will quite naturally be no true likeness of the true God" (*The Knowledge of the Holy* [San Francisco: Harper & Row, 1961], p. 11). Committing idolatry is not just wearing a loincloth and kneeling before an image; therefore, civilized people aren't immune from it. Idolatry is assuming God to be something He is not: to have either unworthy or erroneous views of Him.

Romans 1:21-23 says of the human race: "When they knew God, they glorified him not as God, neither were thankful, but became vain [proud] in their imaginations, and their foolish heart was darkened. Professing themselves to be wise, they became fools, and changed the glory of the incorruptible God into an image made like corruptible man." Man has always wanted to make God in his own image—to drag God down. Any unworthy thought about God is idolatry, but the idolatrous act we commit most frequently is reducing God to our level.

b) The illustrations

(1) Abusing the name of Jesus

Have you noticed that *Jesus* is the most popular name for the second Person of the Trinity? In the charismatic movement it is practically the only name they use. Consequently, in many people's minds He has become a buddy or pal. The full name of the second Person of the Trinity is the *Lord Jesus Christ*. Using the name *Jesus* is not wrong, but we must not humanize our Lord at the expense of His deity in an effort to make Him seem like a buddy. When we no longer conceive of Him as He ought to be conceived of, we are idolaters.

(2) Not trusting in God

Whenever someone fails to trust God, he in a sense commits idolatry. John said, "He that believeth not God hath made him a liar" (1 John 5:10). Consider the Christian who has a problem and, instead of praying about it and trusting God, panics and begins to doubt God. In his mind he has said, "God, I'm not sure You can do what You claim." That's idolatry because he thought unworthily or erroneously of God. Holding to any false teaching concerning the Holy Spirit, Christ, or the Father is tantamount to idolatry, for it makes God something other than He is. Therefore Christians can be guilty of idolatry.

We need to understand that an idolater is not the primitive person who kneels before a rock; *anyone* who entertains thoughts of God that aren't worthy of His character is an idolater. God will not tolerate a man-made god who bears His name.

2. Worshiping the true God in a wrong way

You remember that in an earlier chapter (see pp. 31-32) we discussed the golden calf Paul alludes to in 1 Corinthians 10. We discovered that the Israelites made the golden calf to represent the God who brought them out of Egypt. After Aaron finished the calf, he said, "Tomorrow is a feast to the Lord [Jehovah]" (Ex. 32:5). Psalm 106:19-20 says, "They made a calf in Horeb and worshiped the melted image. Thus they changed their glory into the similitude of an ox that eateth grass." Who is the glory of Israel? Jehovah God. In their thinking they changed God into an ox. If anyone has thoughts less than true of God, in any of the manifestations of His Trinity, he has constituted idolatry. Throughout Israel's history there was that strange intermingling of idolatry with true worship. They were worshiping the true God in the wrong way.

Many people worship God with emotion void of truth. John said one must worship God "in spirit *and in truth*" (John 4:24, emphasis added). Another wrong way to worship is to magnify form and ritual until no one can see the reality of them. When you substitute ceremony for true worship, the product is mindless worship. There are many ways to worship wrongly; Israel did by making a molten image to represent the true God.

Today many worship God apart from truth. And when you do not worship Him in truth, you tend to worship Him from your senses only. The result is sensual worship that translates easily into the pagan worship common in history. Invariably, ancient false religious systems were wed to sexual sin, because their worship was pure experience without the foundation of truth. On the other hand, some, like the Jewish religious leaders in the time of Christ, reduced worship to a cold, dead, formal creed. That also is idolatry, because it is worship of the form rather than the God behind the form.

3. Worshiping any image

Numerous passages develop this theme, but let's consider Isaiah 44, which discusses the stupidity of idolatry. Verses 9-14 describe the making of an idol. In verses 15-16 Isaiah tells of a man who cuts down a tree, uses it for heat and to cook food, then carves an idol from the rest, underscoring the illogical nature of idolatry. Verse 17 says that from "the residue of it [the tree] he maketh a god, even his carved image; he falleth down unto it, and worshipeth it, and prayeth unto it and saith, Deliver me; for thou art my God." That's a clear illustration of idolatry: after a man fashions an image, he worships it as his god. Christians must never substitute an image for reality.

Pictures of Christ

The Bible is clear that we are not to bow down to images. Many people have told me that when they pray, they kneel before a picture of Christ. I believe doing that can seem superstitious and is potentially confusing, but if you keep a proper perspective, kneeling before a picture of Christ isn't necessarily idolatry. Still, we must not worship images of any kind. To assume that there is power in an image is wrong.

4. Worshiping angels

Fortunately we don't know enough about angels to become too involved in worshiping them; we know the names of only three: Satan (Luke 10:18), Gabriel (Luke 1:26), and Michael (Jude 9). In the book of Revelation we read that John tried to worship an angel but immediately the angel said, "See thou do it not; for I am thy fellow servant. . . . Worship God" (22:9). In Colossians 2:18 Paul warns the believers about a false doctrine regarding the worship of angels. Worshiping angels is idolatry.

5. Worshiping devils

Revelation 9:20 says that during the Tribulation people will worship not only idols of stone and wood but also demons. Today many worship in the satanic church and bow down to demons. Others are devoted to false deities, spirit beings, and mediums.

6. Worshiping the dead

Perhaps you have never thought of this, but worshiping the dead is idolatry. Psalm 106:28, describing Israel's typical pattern of unfaithfulness to God, says, "They joined themselves also unto Baal-peor [a form of Baal worship], and ate the sacrifices of the dead." Some scholars believe this is a reference to dead idols as opposed to the living God, rather than a reference to dead men. In either case we are never to worship dead men or dead idols. Jesus said, "Thou shalt worship the Lord, thy God, and him only shalt thou serve" (Matt. 4:10). He is not only the supreme One to be worshiped; He is the *only* One. Who the dead man is doesn't matter. Baal worship often took place in gardens and groves, where the people worshiped graves and monuments that represented the dead. That's idolatry.

7. Being preoccupied with anything other than God

a) Summarized

A form of idolatry much more relevant to our society and attitudes is any idol of the heart. Any thinking person, asked to name the idols he struggles with, would be able to come up with something. If you can't, ask your family—they know what you worship and, frankly, so do you.

Some bow down to education and the pursuit of academic degrees, others to science. Chad Walsh, in *Campus Gods on Trial,* said, "Some of the favorite classroom gods are Progress, Relativism, Scientism, and Humanitarianism" ([New York: Macmillan, 1956], p. xi). Billy Graham capsuled humanism when he said, "We have 'In God we trust' engraved on our coins, but 'Me first' engraved on our hearts" (*World Aflame* [New York: Doubleday, 1965], p. 42). Humanism surfaces in the words of the child who says, "Mother, I would rather do it myself." But one whom humanism has mastered claims he can handle his own problems, solve his own mysteries, and run his own world. Materialism and sex are other gods of humanity. When I visited Baalbek in Lebanon, I saw the temple of orgies, which was dedicated to the god Bacchus—an incredible edifice for worshiping sex, which has always been one of man's gods.

Ezekiel 14:3 says, "Son of man, these men [Israel's elders, cf. v. 1] have set up their idols in their heart, and put the stumbling block of their iniquity before their face." They hadn't made any stone images or gold and silver gods, but they had idols in their heart that blinded them to all else. Men can't give God priority because they're too busy acquiring an education, making money, or being somebody. They're too busy with their activities or with worshiping recreation. Verses 4-5 say, "Thus saith the Lord God: Every man of the house of Israel that setteth up his idols in his heart, and putteth the stumbling block of his iniquity before his face, and cometh to the prophet, I, the Lord, will answer him that cometh according to the multitude of his idols, that I may take the house of Israel in their own heart, because they are estranged from me through their idols." Idolatry consists of any idol in the heart.

b) Specified

Let's be specific about two idols of the heart.

(1) Greed

In Ephesians 5 Paul has established that as God's children, we ought to walk in love, which means to avoid false love but maintain true love. False love consists of fornication and other sins named in verses 3-4. Then in verse 5 he says, "This ye know that no fornicator, nor unclean person, nor covetous man (who is an idolater) hath any inheritance in the kingdom of Christ and of God" (cf. Col. 3:5). Greed is idolatry.

Someone who covets worships materialism, which emphasizes money and possessions. One can covet a house, a car, clothes, money, stocks, a bigger business, or more of anything. Covetousness is wanting what you don't have. Paul said,

"I have learned, in whatever state I am, in this to be content. I know both how to be abased, and I know how to abound" (Phil. 4:11-12). May God help us to attain that level of maturity.

Jesus said you can't worship the true God and money at the same time (Matt. 6:24). In fact, money often interferes with worshiping God. Paul said, "They that will be rich fall into temptation and a snare, and into many foolish and hurtful lusts, which drown men in destruction and perdition" (1 Tim. 6:9). Perhaps, like the idols of Israel's elders, money or possessions have come between you and God, so that you can't see Him anymore.

(2) Lust

Philippians 3:19 speaks of those "whose end is destruction, whose god is their belly, and whose glory is in their shame, who mind earthly things" (KJV). "Belly" could better be translated "appetite," or better, "lust."

Lust can involve the belly. Some people live for one thing: food. They don't finish one meal before they're thinking about the next. Because our society constantly assaults our senses with new tastes, we can lose our perspective and begin living to eat, rather than eating to live.

But eating isn't all that Paul means. The Greek word translated "belly" has a much broader meaning. It is a lust for anything. Some people, for example, go from magazines to television programs to seek sexual gratification. Sex is in their minds all the time. The lust of the eyes, the lust of the flesh, and the pride of life (1 John 2:16) can easily become gods.

Now that we have learned what idolatry is, what are we to do about it? First Corinthians 10:14 says to flee. Paul warned the Corinthians that if they lived on the edge of liberty, they wouldn't recognize the danger. You may believe you can continually indulge your liberty and be unaffected, but if you keep exposing yourself to sin, tragedy is imminent.

III. THE GRIM RESULTS OF IDOLATRY

We ought to run from idolatry because of its effects.

A. It Defiles You

Ezekiel 20:7 says, "Defile not yourselves with idols." Whether they're the gods of Egypt, such as the sun god Ra, or the modern gods of the heart, such as golf or money, idols have a defiling effect. Idolatry circumvents righteousness in all who participate, whether believer or unbeliever. Although God graciously forgives and keeps on cleansing the believer, the sin is no less idolatrous and no less defiling.

B. It Pollutes Others

Idolatry not only defiles the person involved but also pollutes everyone around him. In Israel a small group began worshiping Baal, and soon their idolatry had national consequences. Ezekiel 36:18, clarifying how that group affected the nation, says, "Wherefore, I poured my fury upon them for the blood that they had shed upon the land, and for their idols by which they had polluted it." Whatever the idol, it not only devastates me but pollutes everyone I touch.

C. It Doesn't Help

Idols can't help anyone. When serious problems come, you can't turn to money, education, or fame. A big house or bank account won't help. Isaiah 46 is a satire on idolatry. It describes men who made an idol and set it in place. Verse 7 says, "It standeth; from its place shall it not move; yea, one shall cry unto it, yet can it not answer, nor save him out of his trouble." Idols can't help you.

D. It Brings Judgment

1. Described in Ezekiel

In addition, idols activate God's vengeance. In Ezekiel 44:10 God says, "The Levites that are gone away far from me, when Israel went astray, who went astray away from me after their idols, they shall even bear their iniquity."

2. Described in Isaiah

In Isaiah 65:2-7 God says, "I have spread out my hands all the day unto a rebellious people, that walketh in a way that was not good, after their own thoughts; a people that provoketh me to anger continually to my face; that sacrificeth in gardens, and burneth incense upon altars of brick; that remain among the graves, and lodge in the monuments; that eat swine's flesh, and broth of abominable things is in their vessels; that say, Stand by thyself, come not near to me; for I am holier than thou. These are a smoke in my nose [i.e., they irritate Me], a fire that burneth all the day. Behold, it is written before me; I will not keep silence, but will recompense, even recompense into their bosom. Your iniquities, and the iniquities of your fathers together, saith the Lord, who have burned incense upon the mountains, and blasphemed me upon the hills; therefore will I measure their former work into their bosom." Now that is the result of idolatry: the recompensing vengeance of God. A man who worships any other than the true God, or who worships the true God in a way other than through His Son, will suffer God's retribution.

E. It Destroys Good Judgment

Isaiah 57 adds another result of idolatry. After using words like *sorceress, adulterer,* and *harlot* (v. 3), Isaiah reveals that idols inflame the heart (v. 5). Idols set men on fire and begin to consume them. A man who has a fire in his heart has an uncontrollable passion. Verse 5 speaks of "inflaming yourselves with idols under every green tree." At the spring festivals the Palestinian pagans hung their sacrifices on huge trees and then burned the whole tree. God used that act as a metaphor for the burning of His people's hearts.

Isaiah 57:5 also tells us the people were "slaying the children in the valleys under the clefts of the rocks." As part of their sacrifices to the god Molech, the Ammonites slew children. When they built a building, they would put a live infant in a jar, seal the jar, and insert it into a wall. But here Isaiah is referring to when they tied children in leather bags and threw them off a cliff. That's idolatry at its worst, and Israel was involved in it.

In Jeremiah 50:38 Jeremiah says, "They are mad over their idols." The people lost their senses. A lifetime of worshiping wrong gods or worshiping in wrong ways can cause a man to think and act insanely.

Conclusion

Deuteronomy 7:25 says idolatry "is an abomination to the Lord thy God." Deuteronomy 16:22 says, "Neither shalt thou set thee up any image, which the Lord thy God hateth." In Deuteronomy 17:2-7 God further expresses His attitude by commanding that idolaters be stoned. In Jeremiah 8 God says that idolaters "shall be for refuse upon the face of the earth" (v. 2). In Revelation 21:8 and 22:15 God asserts that no idolater will ever enter His kingdom. The only sensible way to react to idolatry is to run from it.

In his final message to Israel before his death, Joshua told them not to mingle with "these nations, these that remain among you; neither make mention of the name of their gods, nor cause to swear by them, neither serve them, nor bow yourselves unto them. But cleave unto the Lord your God, as ye have done unto this day" (23:7-8). Paul echoed Joshua's words—have nothing to do with idols; don't even talk about them—cling to God. We have liberty in Christ, but not to see how close we can get to the world's idolatry before falling into temptation and sin. Keep running from idolatry!

Focusing on the Facts

1. What issue did the Corinthians' question about meat offered to idols raise (see pp. 58-59)?
2. Explain the conflict between the mature believer and the weak believer concerning meat offered to idols (see p. 59).
3. What two answers does Paul give to the Corinthians' question (see p. 60)?

4. What insight does 1 Corinthians 5:11 give to the situation in the Corinthian church (see pp. 60-61)?
5. What is the thesis of Paul's discussion concerning idolatry? Explain (see p. 61).
6. Why is idolatry a serious sin? Explain (see p. 62).
7. Give a basic definition of idolatry (see p. 62).
8. Explain how a lack of trust can be idolatrous (see p. 63).
9. List several wrong ways to worship God (see p. 64).
10. What is the result of worshiping apart from truth (see p. 64)?
11. The Bible records the names of what angels (see p. 65)?
12. Explain what Ezekiel 14:3 teaches about idolatry (see p. 67).
13. Define covetousness. What does Ephesians 5:5 say about it (see p. 67)?
14. What does "whose God is their belly" mean? How can it be applied (Phil. 3:19; see p. 68)?
15. What effects does idolatry have? Explain each (see pp. 67-71).
16. What is God's attitude toward idolatry? What Scripture passages support that (see p. 71)?

Pondering the Principles

1. Read Romans 1:18-25. Verse 20 details what God has revealed about Himself to mankind. Verse 21 presents two wrong responses of man to that revelation. To what extent do you characterize the opposite responses? Write down man's wrong responses, and then list ways in which you can manifest the opposite today. Decide to respond correctly to God's revelation of Himself.

2. Trust is confidence in or dependence upon someone or something. Since a lack of trust is idolatry, trusting God is essential in our relationship with Him. Think of any areas in which you tend to doubt God or to act independently of Him. Confess that lack of trust as sin, and ask Him to help you trust Him fully. Read and memorize Psalm 62:8 and Proverbs 3:5-6.

5
The Outrage of Idolatry

Outline

Introduction
A. Idolatrous Feasts
B. The Lord's Supper
1. Instituted by the Lord
2. Practiced by the church

Review

Lesson
I. Idolatry Is Inconsistent (vv. 16-18)
A. The Elements of the Lord's Supper (v. 16)
1. The cup (v. 16*a*-*b*)
a) Designated (v. 16*a*)
b) Defined (v. 16*b*)
(1) The meaning of communion
(2) The metonym of blood
2. The bread (v. 16*c*)
a) The background of "body"
b) The humanness of Christ
c) The breaking of the bread
B. The Effect of the Lord's Supper (vv. 17-18)
1. Indicated (v. 17)
2. Illustrated (v. 18)
II. Idolatry Is Demonic (vv. 19-21)
A. It is confusing (v. 19)
B. It is deceptive (v. 20*a*)
C. It is illogical (vv. 20*b*-21)
III. Idolatry Is Offensive to the Lord (v. 22)

Conclusion

Introduction

In 1 Corinthians 10:14-22 Paul talks about idolatry. That subject arose because some Corinthian Christians, in the name of Christian liberty, were attending idolatrous activities. They had concluded that since an idol is nothing—it isn't the god the idolaters believe it is—God is therefore unconcerned about the meaningless rituals that accompany its worship. Consequently, Christians believed their involvement with those rituals would be insignificant and harmless.

A. Idolatrous Feasts

The Corinthians had asked Paul if it was wrong to eat meat offered to idols. In their society meat offerings were made continuously to hundreds of gods, and since an idol is nothing and God isn't concerned about what we eat, some decided they could eat the meat. And if they could eat meat offered to idols, they reasoned that they could attend idolatrous festivals. Some of them were re-entering Corinth's social, economic, political, and cultural life by attending feasts that accompanied idol worship.

Paul's answer to them in verse 14 is clear: "My dearly beloved, flee from idolatry." One must not pursue idolatry in the name of Christian liberty. It may be acceptable to eat meat once offered to idols but bought in a butcher shop or served in a friend's home. But when someone attends idolatrous festivals, he has overextended his liberty. In verses 14-22 Paul explains why a believer should avoid idolatry.

B. The Lord's Supper

He uses the Lord's Supper as the foundation of his argument. In fact, from here throughout most of chapter 11 it is Paul's theme.

1. Instituted by the Lord

The gospels record that the Lord instituted this celebration the night before His crucifixion. Matthew 26 says that "as they were eating, Jesus took bread, and blessed it, and broke it, and gave it to the disciples, and said, Take, eat; this is my body. And he took the cup, and gave thanks, and gave it to them, saying, Drink ye all of it; for this is my blood of the new testament [covenant], which is shed for many for the remission [forgiveness] of sins. But I say unto you, I will not drink henceforth of this fruit of the vine, until that day when I drink it new with you in my Father's kingdom" (vv. 26-29).

While the Lord celebrated the Passover meal with His disciples, which involved four cups of wine, He gave what may have been the third cup a new meaning. Rather than continuing as a memorial of the Exodus, it became a memorial of the Messiah's death. And the Lord's Table has continued as an institution of the church throughout history.

2. Practiced by the church

The birth of the church occurred on the Day of Pentecost. Speaking about that day, Acts 2:41-42 says, "They that gladly received his word were baptized; and the same day there were added unto them about three thousand souls. And they continued steadfastly in the apostles' doctrine [teaching] and fellowship [ministering to one another], and in breaking of bread [Communion], and in prayers." One of the four distinctives of the church was the Lord's Supper. Verse 46 adds that they celebrated it "daily" and "from house to house." And the Lord's Supper continues to unite the church and its Savior, the Lord Jesus Christ. In 1 Corinthians 10–11 the significance of the Lord's Supper becomes the basis of Paul's argument that a believer should avoid idolatry.

Review

Paul confronted the Corinthian Christians, telling them that in the name of liberty they had exposed themselves to idol worship. Because of their self-confidence they were in danger of falling into sin (1 Cor. 10:12). Using a present imperative in verse 14, he tells them to be continually fleeing from idolatry.

Several points summarize what idolatry is. It is slandering God's character—entertaining erroneous or unworthy thoughts about Him. In addition, idolatry is worshiping the true God in a wrong way. When Israel made a golden calf to represent Jehovah, they were worshiping Him in a wrong way. Also, idolatry is worshiping things other than God, such as images, angels, demons, or dead men. According to Ezekiel 14:3, having any idol in the heart, such as money, fame, or prestige, is idolatry.

Lesson

After telling the Corinthians to flee from idolatry, Paul asks them in verse 15 to listen to his argument and judge the validity of his conclusions. "I speak as to wise men; judge ye what I say." Then he gave them three reasons to run from idolatry: it is inconsistent, it is demonic, and it is offensive to the Lord.

I. IDOLATRY IS INCONSISTENT (vv. 16-18)

"The cup of blessing which we bless, is it not the communion of the blood of Christ? The bread which we break, is it not the communion of the body of Christ? For we being many are one bread, and one body; for we are all partakers of that one bread. Behold Israel after the flesh. Are not they who eat of the sacrifices partakers of the altar?"

Paul assumed that a Christian participates regularly in the Lord's Table. That participation is crucial because it continually illustrates the believer's union with his Lord and with all believers. The apostle didn't even entertain the thought that a Christian wouldn't participate. Perhaps you can't attend when your church celebrates the Lord's Supper. You can, however, make time to partake in your home or some other place.

Paul's thought is this: when someone takes the cup and the bread, he is actually communing with Christ (v. 16) and with every other participant (v. 17). Religious feasts and celebrations involve the worshiper with all other worshipers and with the one being worshiped. That's precisely why a Christian shouldn't attend an idolatrous feast. If he goes, he becomes involved, whether willingly or not, with the idol and its worshipers. Both the Lord's Table and an idolatrous feast constitute a real communion of sorts.

A. The Elements of the Lord's Supper (v. 16)

1. The cup (v. 16*a-b*)

a) Designated (v. 16*a*)

"The cup of blessing which we bless."

"The cup of blessing" was the name of the third cup consumed in the Passover feast. On the night before His death the Lord may have used it to institute Communion. But basically "cup of blessing" refers to the cup that Christ Himself had blessed. At the Last Supper Jesus took that cup and "gave thanks [Gk., *eucharisteō,* "to bless" or "to give thanks"]" (Matt. 26:27). He transformed an ordinary cup into something sacred because He set it apart for special use; He blessed it. Paul adds in verse 16 that we bless it also. We do so by thanking God and setting it apart for sacred use.

Therefore "the cup of blessing which we bless" is simply the Communion cup. Today for obvious reasons most churches use many cups instead of one in the communion service. Nevertheless they all are symbols of the one Jesus blessed.

b) Defined (v. 16*b*)

"Is it not the communion of the blood of Christ?"

(1) The meaning of communion

When one drinks the cup at the Lord's Table, he is communing with the blood of Christ. What does that mean? Some interpreters say the cup is a symbol of His blood. The passage, however, says it is much more than a symbol: it is "communion" (Gk., *koinōnia,* "participation"). When we partake of that cup, a spiritual reality occurs—we commune with Christ's death.

For example, when you see a picture of someone you love who has died, it isn't just a picture. As soon as you see it, suddenly everything about that person is alive to you. I look at pictures of friends who have died, and my mind is flooded with memories. Likewise, partaking of Communion actualizes Christ's death—it makes His death for me vivid and real. The cup is more than a symbol: it is a symbol that God's Spirit activates to make Christ's death a living reality to me. It is an actual communion.

(2) The metonym of blood

Before we can understand Paul's reasoning, we must understand the English word *metonym.* The dictionary defines it as "an attribute or commonly associated feature used to name or designate something." It is a word used to designate something because it has an actual relationship with it.

For example, someone might say he was reading Shakespeare. Actually, reading Shakespeare is a literal impossibility; one can't read a person. The reader meant he was reading Shakespeare's writings. Shakespeare's name can be a metonym for his writings because his name is closely associated with them.

The term *blood* substitutes for the term *death.* "The blood of Christ" is a metonym for "the death of Christ." Scripture uses that metonym because to the Hebrew the shedding of blood brought to mind a violent death.

Blood: The Symbol of His Violent Death

There was nothing in the chemistry of Christ's literal blood that was efficacious for removing sin. The Bible doesn't teach that the blood itself can save us, nor does it even emphasize the actual blood. Instead it stresses the shedding or pouring out of His blood, emblematic of His violent death. Romans 6:23 says, "The wages of sin is death." His death paid the price for our salvation. The Hebrew Christians spoke of His shed blood because it speaks of violent death. Leviticus 17:11 says that "the life of the flesh is in the blood." The pouring out of blood connotes death.

"Communion of the blood of Christ" doesn't suggest that the literal blood of Christ is efficacious. It means that we enter into a genuine, vital participation in His death. Partaking of the cup that Jesus blessed is an act of communion with the death of Christ.

2. The bread (v. 16*c*)

"The bread [loaf] which we break, is it not the communion of the body of Christ?"

a) The background of "body"

At the Last Supper the Lord said of the bread, "This is my body which is given for you" (Luke 22:19). In the Hebrew mind the word *body* referred to our humanness and the totality of earthy life. The Hebrew word for earth is *adamah,* and the word for man is *adam.* God used the earth to form the body—*adam* came from *adamah.*

b) The humanness of Christ

Paul is saying here that to eat the bread is to commune with the Body of Christ. "Body of Christ" is not primarily a reference to the cross. By the bread we remember and commune with our Lord's incarnation. We remember Him as a sympathetic High Priest as well as a bleeding, dying Savior. Communion relates us to the living Christ, "who, although He existed in the form of God, did not regard equality with God a thing to be grasped, but emptied Himself, taking the form of a bond-servant, and being made in the likeness of men. And being found in appearance as a man, He humbled Himself by becoming obedient to the point of death, even death on a cross" (Phil. 2:6-8, NASB). He purposed to become a sympathetic high priest who "was in all points tempted like as we are, yet without sin" (Heb. 4:15).

c) The breaking of the bread

The bread reminds us of His life, of His humanness. God gave Himself to us as a human being to suffer what we suffer, hurt where we hurt, and be tempted as we're tempted. He indeed is our sympathetic high priest. The breaking of the loaf does not refer to the cross primarily although, as part of His human suffering, it is certainly included. The loaf is simply a symbol of His humanness.

The breaking of it has no symbolic connection to the cross. People often say that the Lord's body was broken on the cross, but the Bible specifically declares it was not. John 19 tells us Jesus died before the Sabbath began and thus avoided having His legs broken to speed up the process of death. Verse 36 says "these things were done, that the scripture should be fulfilled, A bone of him shall not be broken."

The only reason Jesus broke the loaf was to give everyone a piece of it. First Corinthians 10:17 says, "We are all partakers of that one bread." His body was never broken; breaking refers only to the distribution of that one loaf, communicating that all believers share in His life. We commune not only with Christ's death but also with His life. In Philippians 3:10 Paul says, "That I may know him, and the power of his resurrection [a reference to His death], and the fellowship of his sufferings [a reference to His life], being made conformable unto his death." In a sense he wanted the humanity of Jesus relived in him. He wanted to bear the marks of Jesus in his body (Gal. 6:17), enduring the sufferings meant for Him (Col. 1:24). He wanted to commune with Christ's humanness. He desired to be persecuted for righteousness' sake, as Christ was, and find in Him a sympathetic high priest who knows everything that we suffer because He suffered it Himself.

Communion—An Awareness of Christ's Presence

The elements of bread and wine are not merely symbols. When we partake, an actual communion occurs. "Communion" (Gk., *koinōnia*) means "participation," "partnership," or "fellowship." As Christians we literally participate in Christ. First Corinthians 1:9 refers to "the fellowship of his Son," 2 Corinthians 13:14 to "the communion of the Holy Spirit" (cf. Phil. 2:1), 2 Corinthians 8:4 to "the fellowship of the ministering to the saints," Philippians 1:5 to "your fellowship in the gospel," and Philippians 3:10 to "the fellowship of his sufferings." We constantly fellowship with Christ, sharing His Spirit, His ministry, His gospel, and His sufferings. And in the Lord's Supper we share the meaning, benefits, and purpose of His death.

When someone partakes of the cup and the bread, he suddenly is sensitized to the reality of what Christ went through on our behalf. He understands that Christ lived, suffered, and became a sympathetic High Priest. All those truths become more real during Communion.

The same effect results from reading your Bible. Although Christ is actively with you whether you are with other believers or are alone, you may have spent a whole day totally unaware of His presence. But because "the word of God is living" (Heb. 4:12), Christ suddenly becomes real to you as you read it. He had been present all the time, but you were not sensitized to it. Or perhaps after being busy with life's responsibilities, you began to pray and became intensely aware of the Lord's presence, which was actually with you all the time.

That is exactly what Communion does. A believer sees the symbol, and his mind begins to perceive the reality behind it. He realizes that Christ is alive and that He carries our cares. He realizes that Christ died for our sins so that we don't have to bear the penalty for them. What is forever true about Christ is sensitively brought to mind in Communion.

B. The Effect of the Lord's Supper (vv. 17-18)

Paul informed the Corinthians that when they came to the Lord's Table, they communed with Christ and actively partook of all that He is and has done. However, that means that when they attended idolatrous festivals, ate food offered to an idol, and fellowshiped with idolaters, they were identifying themselves with that idol. Communing with Christ and with idols is hopelessly inconsistent.

1. Indicated (v. 17, NASB)

   "Since there is one bread, we who are many are one body; for we all partake of the one bread."

   Because there's only one bread, which is Christ, everyone who partakes of it is one with every other partaker. We are all one body and partake of one loaf. We are inseparably joined not only to Christ but also to each other.

2. Illustrated (v. 18)

   "Behold Israel after the flesh. Are not they who eat of the sacrifices partakers of the altar?"

   The altar refers to the worship of God. Paul was referring to the Jewish sacrificial system. Whenever an Israelite offered his sacrifice, part of it was offered to God. The priests, other worshipers, and the one who made the sacrifice shared the rest.

   Participation in religious rites has deep spiritual meaning, because it implies a union between the worshipers and the one being worshiped. You can't participate in idolatrous rites casually. Israel's sacrifices were shared. Paul's point is that worship is an identification and communion with whomever is being worshiped! For the Jewish people, communion with the altar meant fellowship with God and everyone else at the altar. For Christians, communion with Christ at the Lord's Supper means fellowship with Christ and everyone else at His Table.

As Christians we can't participate in any of the idolatrous, Christless activities of our world without becoming identified with them and becoming one with everyone involved. Some Christians believe they can attend wild parties and stay detached, but actually they are one with whatever happens and are identified with it. You have liberty. But if your liberty drags you into communion with the world and its satanic system, you need to pull away.

II. IDOLATRY IS DEMONIC (vv. 19-21)

"What say I, then? That the idol is anything, or that which is offered in sacrifice to idols is anything? But I say that the things which the Gentiles sacrifice, they sacrifice to demons, and not to God; and I would not that ye should have fellowship with demons. Ye cannot drink the cup of the Lord, and the cup of demons; ye cannot be partakers of the Lord's table, and of the table of demons."

A. It is confusing (v. 19)

"What say I, then? That the idol is anything, or that which is offered in sacrifice to idols is anything?"

Paul feared that the believers in Corinth would be confused, thinking he was saying that an idol is really a god and that a sacrifice to it is meaningful. But in verse 4 of chapter 8 he says that an idol is nothing and in verse 8 that the food offered to an idol is nothing. He wanted them to understand that if they commune with an idol, they are not communing with another god because there are no other gods. Still, a communion of some kind exists—a communion with demons.

B. It is deceptive (v. 20*a*)

"But I say that the things which the Gentiles sacrifice, they sacrifice to demons, and not to God."

An idol is not a god, but if someone wants to believe it is, Satan will send a demon to impersonate the god that the person believes is there. And that demon will do enough tricks to keep him worshiping that idol. Why would somebody in another society worship a rock? Because a demon who impersonates it does enough to keep him believing that the rock is a god. Why do people follow astrology? Because demons make enough predictions come true to hook those people. Why do people stay in false religious systems and never see the truth? Because they have seen supernatural revelations in those systems. Idols are not gods, but demons will impersonate them.

Idolatry constitutes demonic communion. When a Christian worships in a false religious system or becomes a part of it by his presence, he communes with demons and the worshipers of demons. Paul's point is that idolatry is demonic. Because Satan is the prince of this world, his demons impersonate the gods of all the evil religious systems of the world and maintain those systems.

According to the Septuagint, the Greek translation of the Hebrew Old Testament, Psalm 96:5 (which is Psalm 95:5 in the Septuagint) says, "All the gods of the nations are demons" (cf. Deut. 32:17; Psalm 106:37). If a person worships a false god, a demon will impersonate it.

C. It is illogical (vv. 20*b*-21)

"I would not that ye should have fellowship with demons. Ye cannot drink the cup of the Lord, and the cup of demons; ye cannot be partakers of the Lord's table, and of the table of demons."

If a Christian who is communing with the Lord through the cup and the bread goes to an idol feast and participates, he is communing with demons. Paul tells them that he doesn't want them to have fellowship with demons. A person cannot—the cannot of consistency, not of impossibility—be consistent and drink the cup of the Lord and the cup of demons. He cannot partake of the Lord's Table and the table of demons. Doing so would be inconsistent.

All idolatry—whether it's libel against God's character, the worship of an image, covetousness, lust, or idols in the heart—it is all demonic. I believe demons can influence us as Christians when our wrong choices give them an open door. In the New Testament demons severely harmed believers on two occasions. Ananias and Sapphira, under the influence of Satan, willfully sinned against the Holy Spirit without confessing or repenting and lost their lives (Acts 5:1-11). And here the Corinthians stayed so close to the world's systems that they were communing with demons. Communing with demons is not impossible for a Christian to do, but doing so is inconsistent and will produce terrible results.

That's why John said, "If there come any unto you, and bring not this doctrine, receive him not into your house, neither bid him Godspeed; for he that biddeth him Godspeed is partaker [Gk., *koinōneō*] of his evil deeds" (2 John 10-11). If you let a false teacher into your house, you are communing with him. Don't do that! Although some believe they can commune with Christ and pursue sinful activities, all believers must be sure that their communion is holy and purely identified with Jesus Christ, not demons.

III. IDOLATRY IS OFFENSIVE TO THE LORD (v. 22)

"Do we provoke the Lord to jealousy? Are we stronger than he?"

A wise man doesn't make enemies of people who are stronger than he is. Paul is saying, "I don't ever want to irritate God!" In Deuteronomy 32:21 God says, "They have moved me to jealousy with that which is not God; they have provoked me to anger with their vanities." Never stir God to jealousy with idolatry because the Bible reveals that He deals strongly with those who do. Deuteronomy 7:1-11; 17:2-7; Jeremiah 25:1-11; 44:1-28; and Revelation 14:9-20; 21:8; and 22:14-15 reveal the vengeance of God against idolaters. Don't provoke God to jealousy. Idolatry is offensive to the Lord, and no idolater has ever escaped His judgment. Scripture says idolaters will have no part in His kingdom (Rev. 21:8; 22:15).

Conclusion

We are free in Christ, but we have to consider how our freedom will affect others and how it will affect us. We must not offend others or expose ourselves to idolatry, sin, and ultimately the chastisement of God. I reiterate what the apostle John said at the end of his first epistle: "Little children, keep yourselves from idols" (1 John 5:21).

Focusing on the Facts

1. Explain why the Corinthian Christians believed their involvement with idolatrous rituals was insignificant (see p. 74).
2. What change did the Lord make in the significance of the Passover celebration (see p. 75)?
3. What event heralded the birth of the church (see p. 75)?
4. What are four distinctives of the early church (Acts 2:41-42; see p. 75)?
5. What is the basis of Paul's argument that a believer should avoid idolatry? Explain (see p. 75).
6. Summarize Paul's argument in 1 Corinthians 10:16-17 (see pp. 76-77).
7. What is "the cup of blessing" (1 Cor. 10:16; see p. 77)?
8. The cup is much more than a ____________: it is ____________. Explain that statement (see p. 77).
9. What is a metonym? What is "the blood of Christ" a metonym for (see p. 78)?
10. What about Christ does "the Body of Christ" remind us of (see p. 80)?
11. What did Christ's breaking of the bread signify (see p. 80)?
12. Describe the communion that occurs when someone partakes of the cup and the bread (see p. 81).
13. Whenever someone worships, with whom does he commune (see p. 82)?
14. Explain how demons are involved in idolatry (see pp. 83-84).
15. What are two New Testament illustrations of believers who were influenced by demons (see pp. 84-85)?
16. All believers must be sure that their communion is __________, and ________________ ________________ with Christ (see p. 85).
17. What do Revelation 21:8 and 22:15 teach about idolaters (see p. 85)?

Pondering the Principles

1. Acts 2:42 describes some distinctives of the early church, such as continuing in the apostles' teaching, ministering to the saints, partaking of the Lord's Supper, and praying. To what extent do those distinctives characterize your life? List several practical

ways to emulate each. What can you do to strengthen those traits in your church?

2. Read Isaiah 40, noting the comparison of idols to our great God. Take time to meditate on the greatness of God as Isaiah describes Him. Express worship and praise to God for who He is and how He acts toward us. Pay careful attention to Isaiah's contrast between the majesty of God and His tenderness (e.g., vv. 11-12). Think of one person whom you can tell about your God this week.

Scripture Index

Topical Index